Join Our Hearts

Becoming One in The Spirit

by

Stephen Abbott

Marshall Pickering

Marshall Morgan and Scott
Marshall Pickering
34–42 Cleveland Street, London, W1P 5FB, U.K.

Copyright © 1989 Stephen Abbott

First published in 1989 by Marshall Morgan and Scott Publications Ltd
Part of the Marshall Pickering Holdings Group

ISBN: 0 551 01841–0

Text set in Baskerville by Selectmove
Printed in Great Britain at
The Camelot Press Ltd, Southampton

Acknowledgments

I should like first to thank my friend Colin Whittaker, without whose encouragement this book would never have been written, and Bishop George Carey and Roger Forster. Next, I must gratefully acknowledge all those who kindly gave their time to me, either by granting an interview or by writing a letter. These include (in alphabetical order): Anthony Bush, Vic Barron, Clive Calver, Charlie Colchester, Colin Davey, Bob Dunnett, Charlotte Fisher, Clifford Hill, David Holloway, Graham Loader, Brian Mills, Philip Mohabir, Marion Morgan, Robert Scott-Cook, Ron Smith, John Stott, John Turner, and John, John and Graham (clergy of 'Littletown'). My thanks also go to Jane Bartholomew, for her invaluable help with typing. I am most grateful to my church, the Fellowship of the King, Bristol, for generously granting me a sabbatical of three months in which to complete the bulk of the writing. My deepest thanks are due to my wife and children for their love, support and patience as I have wrestled with my ideas and my notes, and, finally, to God, for his inexhaustible grace.

To Val, who has taught me more than anyone else (apart from God) about unity of heart.

Contents

Foreword

Let us be honest about it; ecumenism is considered by most people as a big bore. It is associated with erudite theologians who are out of touch with ordinary Christians and with seemingly irrelevant arguments of bygone days.

What is exciting about this book is that Stephen Abbott makes the subject of unity accessible to us all. He outlines the shape of a biblical ecumenism and puts this in an evangelical and charismatic context. Thereby supplying a missing ingredient in present-day studies of unity for, as far as I can tell, up to now ecumenism has largely been the province of mainstream denominations. Evangelicals have not been significant in this story. Of even greater interest is the fact that Mr Abbott has supplied us with a thoughtful and significant contribution from within the House Church movement; a movement often considered exclusive, fundamentalist and naïve.

But central to the author's concern is that unity is essential because it is at the heart of God himself and is necessary for our mission in the world. There used to be a mocking Muslim saying in African: 'Find ten Christians and you will have eleven different sets of opinions!' How sad it is that others see an unreconciled and divided Christianity where unity in the Gospel should have been visible!

Not all readers will agree with the substance of this book or its conclusions but it will challenge a number of our conclusions and we shall not be the worse for that. In my opinion *Join our Hearts* is an invitation to build our schemes of unity on a sturdy spiritual foundation. Anything else is bound either to fail or to fall short of God's ideal for us his people.

George Bath & Wells

Foreword

I love Christian denominations, movements and streams, I wish there were more of them!

If that sounds extreme in these days of ecumenism consider the alternative. One huge monolithic, totalitarian, worldwide, structure with all the pretensions and corruption which power inevitably brings, calling itself 'the church'. Fortunately history has never been able to produce this nightmare but where there have been partial, limited, local and often mediaeval attempts to create this monster, we have seen enough to be warned!

Of course we are to love one another as Christ loved us. This is the true badge of discipleship. Loving one another across our structural barriers is more realistic, demanding, and some of us believe more scriptural and in tune with Christ's mind, than contriving structural mergers embracing unreconciled Christians. Our structural organisations have been sincerely produced to preserve and promulgate our cherished traditions and valued distinctives and thereby serve the life of Christ in His people. They are not themselves that life and therefore are not the body or indeed the church. They serve the body which is the gift of Jesus to his people. Anyone can love his own type, says Jesus. Loving those who are different from us is the proof of grace. The gift of His body and its unity which Jesus gave us at the last supper is not for us to recreate. Nor are we to talk pretentiously about answering Jesus' prayer for oneness in that same supper. Prayer is to God and answered by Him not us. God answered Jesus' prayer a few hours later when He died and destroyed all of humanity's sinful barriers at the cross and gave us His new humanity and its unity. Our task is to keep this unity not make it, to express it by the ways we love, not organise it bureaucratically.

Structural division will always be with us. At its best

it may reflect the variety and diversity of a triune God. Our supernatural and spiritual unity is not necessarily best expressed by a unification structure. However our love for each other must be visible in order that the world might see our oneness and believe. This book will help us to do that very thing as it enables us to see more clearly what God is doing in and through our denominations today. God is showing that our divisions, which often are barriers, may be treated as distinctives which are challenges, inspiring us to find exciting ways of expressing our unifying love to one another. The true art of a man and a woman making love is found in discovering ways of expressing oneness across the differences of the sexes. This analogy illuminates and illustrates our church scene today and Stephen Abbott has written to help us to engage excitingly in this church process of reaching across our denominational differences. It is a book whose contents I would have been pleased to have written myself. Fortunately for us readers he has beaten me to it and made a far better job than I could ever have done, appealing for us to 'join our hearts'.

Read on in order to know how to participate more fully than ever before in God's exciting adventure of church oneness, with the ultimate objective that the world might thereby be able to believe in our Lord Jesus and that at last His Kingdom might come.

Roger Forster

PART I

Getting the Vision

Chapter 1

Good News or Dirty Word?

A joyful procession of 400 singing people winds its
way through the streets of a residential area of Bristol.
Mothers and children, chatting in doorways, look up
with interest as it approaches. The words of the song,
amplified through a PA system mounted on a lorry,
come through loud and clear:

> Make way, make way, for Christ the king
> In splendour arrives.
> Fling wide the gates and welcome him
> Into your lives.[1]

Stewards hand out leaflets with details of the local
churches and their services. Marchers carry streamers
and balloons. The procession involves Christians from
every church in the area, and includes an assortment
of local ministers, some in their dog-collars. Eventually,
it reaches the park where the marchers mingle with
the crowds of people enjoying themselves on a fine
May afternoon. There is drama, dancing, and a short
address, given from the lorry by one of the vicars.
I find myself standing next to a friend of mine, a
Roman Catholic, who, like me, had been marching in
the procession. She turns to me with a gleam in her eye,
and remarks, 'This is the best thing that has happened
since "Mission England".'

The scene changes. It is six thirty a.m. I arrive at a
house a few minutes' drive away, and push open the
door that has been left on the latch. My host greets me
warmly, if a trifle sleepily. Gradually, the living-room
begins to fill up until there are nine people present. We
start to sing and pray, concentrating our intercession on
the city of Bristol, where we all live. Today, the theme
that God seems to be putting on our hearts is *unity*. 'Lord,
forgive your people for the lack of love between us. Join

3

our hearts together and make us one.' As we pray, I am conscious that we represent at least five different churches, and as many different denominations. We feel the presence of God, and know that, at any rate in this gathering, we are one in the spirit.

The scene shifts again to the home of another of my friends, the leader of a thriving new church in another part of Bristol. The living-room begins to fill up with leaders of various churches in the city, again represent-ing different denominations, who have come to pray for God's guidance. After an hour of worship and prayer, during which we hear God speaking clearly to us, one of the men, a mature and deeply respected pastor, opens up some of the needs of his own church, which has been going through a rocky period. Immediately, we gather round him, lay hands on him, and pray that God will bless him and his church, bringing healing, unity, and a new sense of direction.

'How good and pleasant it is when brothers live together in unity!' (Ps.133.1). The scenes that I have just described give a glimpse of what is wonderfully happening, not just in Bristol, but in every area, town and city in Britain today. Christians are coming together to worship, pray and witness in a way that has probably not happened for many years. Those of us who have experienced something of this know the truth of what King David wrote in that psalm. We know too that in the last verse, he firmly states that in the place where unity has been established among God's people, 'there God bestows his blessing, even life for evermore'. We want God's blessing. We want to experience that quality of eternal life now, in this life. True unity certainly brings that blessing, and we know it.

Yet as we acknowledge blessing, we have to be realistic and admit that there is also, sadly, a great deal of strife on the Christian scene in Britain today. Within churches, where there ought to be peace and harmony, there is frequently bitterness, resentment, jealousy and unforgiveness. Between churches, there is suspicion: of success and size and status, of theological stance, of order and practice. Catholics and Protestants, conservatives and liberals, charismatics and non-charismatics, House Churches and historic denominations should be trying respectfully to understand and love each other (while healthily questioning each other's views and practices) within the rich diversity of Christian understanding and practice that there is in this country. Instead, we so often simply squabble with and denounce each other, in ways which must seem extraordinary, if not irrelevant, to the 90 per cent or so of the population who have no church connection at all.

On the other hand, tragically, the whole idea of 'Christian unity', 'church unity' or 'ecumenism' can put many people off. A few fictional examples will illustrate the point:

Sue sighs at the thought of the council of churches' meeting tonight. The agenda looks as boring and predictable as ever: joint One World Week service, joint carol singing, joint service for the Week of Prayer for Christian Unity. Why don't more than a handful of each congregation turn up to these events? Probably because they're something extra, tacked on to an already busy church programme. Sue cherishes Jesus' prayer in John chapter 17 that 'they may all be one'; it has so often motivated her to carry on when her zeal has begun to flag. Then she notices two items on the agenda that have a different look. 'Lent groups' – well, they were good in 1986 and 1988, very interesting in fact. And what about 'Joint Mission'? Frank from the Baptist church wants to bring that up; he's a bit too evangelical for Sue, but very sincere. It might do the churches some good to reach out to the neighbourhood. But how? Sue thinks of an open-air meeting she encountered one day in the local shopping centre, and shudders. No, she definitely couldn't get involved in anything like that. All the same . . . perhaps tonight's meeting might be a little livelier than usual.

Helen has been at the Living Waters Fellowship for two years now. She left her Baptist church because the minister was totally closed to the gifts of the Holy Spirit.

5

For her, LWF has got it all: wonderful, free worship (with dancing positively encouraged), anointed leadership, close friendships, a sense of God really moving in the church. In fact, Helen can't really understand why anyone should want to go to any church other than LWF. It's so clearly the best church in town. The leaders teach that denominationalism is unscriptural. Helen knows that even lively traditional churches can't ultimately flourish because they're trying to put new wine into old wineskins. In fact, Helen is certain that she's in the right place, in the only church in town that's really going on with God. As for the council of churches – what's the point of belonging to that?

John belongs to Bethel, a chapel where a very particular interpretation of the Scriptures is taught. He feels secure that he is a member of the true church, but is not at all sure about Christians who worship elsewhere. As for the ecumenical movement! It has a whiff of the Pit about it. It's full of liberalism and doctrinal compromise, and it flirts dangerously with Popery. It's probably the start of the counterfeit church prophesied in Revelation chapter 13. He wouldn't for a moment dream of going to a joint prayer-meeting even with the members of the evangelical Anglican church down the road, for isn't the Church of England dangerously compromised, a 'mixed denomination'? He might have to pray with people who aren't really born again, and then he would be 'guilty by association'. Besides, his own cherished beliefs might be called into question.

These deliberately exaggerated case studies highlight three negative reactions to Christians unity:

Unity to Sue seems *boring*. Nothing new or significant ever happens in the search for unity (although there are two items on the agenda that look promising). Only an average of 5 per cent of any given congregation participate in ecumenical events. This poses the question: How can unity be made more interesting?

Unity to Helen seems *irrelevant*. If you are in a church which is going places, why bother with other churches that aren't? The question posed is: How can unity be made important?

Unity to John seems *wrong*. If you are a member of a narrowly exclusive church, you will probably find the adventure of unity extremely threatening. The question posed is: How can unity be shown to be good and right, part of God's will for the church?

The answers must lie in seeing unity from God's perspective. Let's look at a passage of Scripture that is vital for any consideration of unity: the end of Jesus' prayer in John chapter 17, verses 20 to 23, his so-called 'High-Priestly' prayer. Here, he prays for the unity of God's people, 'those who will believe in me through their (the disciples') message, that all of them may be one, Father, just as you are in me and I am in you.' Three points stand out:

First, Jesus' prayer includes us, this generation of Christians, as well as every other intervening generation. He was praying for disciples, people who would commit themselves to him and follow him wherever he led. We need to take his prayer seriously. He wants to help us to fulfil it in our own day, because his purposes never change.

Second, the purpose of his prayer was that we should be one, just as he and the Father were (and are) one. We cannot imagine a closer unity than that. Jesus was not praying for unity on a purely human level, e.g. the unity that exists between friends or within families. What he had in mind was *perfect* unity. That fundamental unity or *oneness* between Christians can only be achieved if they are united in God. Jesus goes on to pray (John 17.21b), 'May they also be in us so that the world may believe that you have sent me.' The purpose of his prayer was that we should be one in the Father and the Son (and, by implication, the Holy Spirit). Christian unity isn't based on a warm glow of emotion, or on friendship (though this is helpful), or on right doctrine (though it is vital for Christians to agree on their understanding of biblical truth). It is based on the unity of relationship that exists within the Trinity. God himself is a model of unity.

Three persons, Father, Son and Holy Spirit, make up one God, in a perfect and eternal relationship of love. The implication of Jesus' prayer is that if we are in a deep and enduring relationship with God, we will be drawn first into the eternal love-relationship of the Trinity, and then into similarly deep and enduring relationships with all other Christians. We might say that a 'vertical unity' with God leads to a 'horizontal unity' with one another.

The word Jesus uses to describe the quality of unity he had in mind is 'glory'. 'I have given them the glory that you gave me, that they may be one as we are one' (John 17.22). God's glory is his pure, uncreated light shining out into the dark world. When Jesus became a man, he brought that glory with him. He showed it through his character, his actions and his teaching – e.g. his love, compassion, wisdom, miracles and goodness. Now, he states that he has chosen to share it with his disciples. It follows that all Jesus' followers can know unity in so far as they partake of his glory, showing it in practical ways through the power of the Holy Spirit working in their lives. As Christians 'remain in Christ' (John 15.4) and 'live by the Spirit' (Gal. 5.16), they will show God's glory, and be increasingly united. This means that unity is neither boring, irrelevant, nor wrong, but glorious!

The third and final point to be drawn from John chapter 17 is that our unity is intended to have an evangelistic purpose. Jesus underlines this point by making it twice: 'May they be in us so that the world may believe that you have sent me' (v.21), and 'May they be brought to complete unity to let the world know that you sent me and have loved them even as you have loved me' (v.22). A unity between Christians that is brought about by the Holy Spirit mediating the love of Christ will have a powerful effect in preaching the good news about Jesus. It will speak at least as loud as, if not louder than, words. On the other hand, disunity and lack of love between Christians will act as a powerful deterrent to those who are seeking God in the Church. Talk of love will appear a sham if it does not really exist between Christians. The world is quick to sniff out and denounce hypocrisy. Disunity deeply dishonours God and the Gospel.

Jesus did not simply pray for unity: he went on to achieve it. Less than twenty-four hours after praying, he had died on the cross to reconcile men and women not only to God – though that was his most important aim – but also to one another (John 11.51–2). After his resurrection, we see the disciples united in joy and wonder in the upper room as Jesus appears to them (Luke 24.36–43, John 20.19–20). After his ascension, they unite in expectant worship and prayer (Luke 24.53, Acts 1.14). Finally, with the coming of the Holy Spirit at Pentecost we see a new, redeemed community spring into life, where the unity that Christ had achieved was experienced and lived out for all to see.

It is clear, then, that true Christian unity is not a grey, wishy-washy, lowest-common-denominator 'fudge'. It is the highest, most glorious, most spirit-filled oneness which God alone can create among Christians who are actually hearing him and obeying him. It is an ideal at which Christians should aim, but which we can only attain with the help of God. Along the way we will achieve a measure of unity. We may be happy about this at the time, but we must never be satisfied with it.

This sort of unity has been to some extent achieved throughout church history, for example in the fervour at the start of monastic movements and religious orders, in the 'radical reformation' of the Anabaptists, in early Methodism and the many other revivals of the past two centuries, and occasionally both in 'charismatic renewal'[2] and in great evangelistic campaigns in our own nation in the last twenty-five years. Those who have experienced a fresh touch from God in these different movements have usually been distinguished by their fervour, purity of doctrine, holiness of life, spontaneity of worship, openness to the Holy Spirit, and many other similar features, as well as by their unity.

It has been possible for some revived groups to stay within the traditional Church structure by forming

9

themselves into religious communities (as in monasticism), but many have felt compelled or seen fit to move outside it. They have split off from the main body of the church in order to achieve the most united grouping (within themselves) possible, and at the same time to remain true to the high calling of God. Such groups have usually been considered heretical, and have often suffered persecution. It is only since the Reformation, chiefly in the last 200 years, that revival movements have been able to flourish unmolested both within and outside the established Church.

For a model of a perfectly united church, we are drawn back to the Jerusalem church described in Acts chapter 2, verses 42 to 47. Many Christians see its structures and characteristics as being unique and unrepeatable, intended by God to empower the church so that Christianity should 'get off the runway'. But no hint of such an interpretation is given in the New Testament. Every positive feature which marks the Jerusalem church can be seen in other local churches mentioned there. History confirms the view that these characteristics have reappeared during subsequent revivals.

In Chapter 3 we shall examine the Jerusalem church in detail. For the purposes of this book, its outstanding feature is the *unity of its members*. In Acts chapter 4, verse 32, we read, 'All the believers were one in heart and mind.' 'Heart' refers to the will, emotions and spirit, i.e. the deepest part of the human personality. 'Mind' (literally 'soul') probably has an almost identical meaning.[3] This depth of unity was an immediate answer to the High-Priestly prayer of Jesus, and it was a direct result of the coming of the Holy Spirit at Pentecost, joining the hearts of the believers in fellowship (Acts 2.42).

The theme of unity continues through the letters of Paul. He is continually urging the churches to seek and express it. He prays for the Romans, 'May the God who gives endurance and encouragement give you a spirit of unity among yourselves, as you follow Christ Jesus, so that with one heart and mouth you may glorify the

God and Father of our Lord Jesus Christ' (Romans 15.6). The Philippians are exhorted to make his joy complete 'by being like-minded, having the same love, being one in spirit and purpose' (Phil. 2.2). Literally, Paul asks them to 'set their minds on the same thing'. The word for 'to set one's mind' does not indicate a merely intellectual process, but an act of the will.[4] In I Corinthians chapter 1, verse 10, he appeals to the Corinthians to 'agree with one another so that there may be no divisions among you and that you may be perfectly united in mind and thought.' Here Paul uses yet another word for 'mind', but again, he does not mean simply an intellectual process – the word connotes *spiritual* knowledge and insight.[5] The basis of our unity as Christians is that we all share in 'the mind of Christ' (I Cor. 2.16) – i.e. in the plans and purposes of the Lord. Our unity is grounded entirely on our relationship with him. 'Unity of mind', when it is seen to be 'in Christ', is simply another aspect of unity of heart.

It is this quality of unity that God still desires for his church. Sometimes it seems that we are light-years away from it! Yet there are signs that Christians in England are beginning to feel the Holy Spirit drawing them together in a new way, as he blows in the churches bringing renewal and, perhaps, the first stirrings of revival. In this book, I look first at the scriptural basis for unity – God's blueprint. Then I examine the history of denominations, some of the main divisions within the church, and moves towards unity at a national level in England (I am not looking at the situations in Scotland, Wales and Northern Ireland, each of which is unique). Finally, I suggest some ways in which true unity of heart can be achieved, and look forward to the full unity to which God is calling his church.

But first, I need to give definitions of three words which will often appear in the following pages:

An *evangelical* is a Christian who holds to the traditional credal doctrinal statements of the church, recognises Scripture as the inspired and authoritative word of God, and believes that mankind is 'fallen', i.e. polluted

11

by sin. Evangelicals also believe that to be 'saved' or freed from sin's power, an individual has to entrust himself to Jesus Christ as the one who has saved us through dying on the cross and rising from the tomb. To receive the benefits of salvation (which include, among other things, personal holiness, the love and power of God, and eternal life), that individual response of faith is vital. Most evangelicals are Protestants, but increasingly there are Roman Catholics (and Orthodox) with strong evangelical leanings.

A *liberal* in theological parlance (not in politics!) is a Christian who does not base his doctrine so much on the Bible direct as upon a particular interpretation of it which appears to be more scientific, psychologically sound, reasonable or comprehensible than the obvious one. This might even mean rejecting parts of the Bible which do not fit into his view of what God, people or the world are like. It may also cause him to re-interpret or reject parts of the creeds, and to believe in universal salvation regardless of whether individuals put their faith in Jesus. Theological liberalism (also called 'modernism')[6] affects many Christians, both Protestant and Roman Catholic.

Finally, the word *charismatic*, derived from the Greek *charisma* meaning a gift of God's grace, is used to denote a Christian who believes that the supernatural gifts of the Holy Spirit listed in I Corinthians, chapter 12, verse 8 to 10, are still in operation today. These include, among others, healing, miracles, tongues, interpretation, and prophecy. Charismatics are to be found in every denomination. Many are evangelical Protestants, though there is a large contingent of Roman Catholic charismatics.

But before moving to the main theme, it may be helpful to devote one chapter to my own spiritual pilgrimage: who I am, where I come from, and what has led me to write this book. In fact, my situation bridges the gap between the more traditional denominations and the new 'house churches', and gives me an unusual – perhaps unique – perspective on Christian unity.

Chapter 2

My Story

I grew up as an Anglican in a wholly Anglican environment. My father was headmaster of Hutton Grammar School in Lancashire at the time that I was born. My earliest recollection of worship was going to Matins in our village church. The boys from the school boarding house occupied a whole section of the church, while I was in a pew with my parents at the front. My mother had a very sensible method of keeping me happy and quiet: she cut up a Mars bar into very small pieces and fed it to me at regular intervals throughout the service.

Later, when I was seven years old, my father retired and we moved south to Bishop's Stortford, where we joined the main parish church, St Michael's. It had a fine choir, of which I became a keen member. We had to sing anthems and special settings of the canticles, and I loved choir practice night. Church to me was very much connected with Anglican church music, and this love has persisted. I cannot say that I very often heard an evangelistic address at St Michael's, biblically-based though the preaching was. One talk, however, stood out as an exception. A visiting speaker showed us Holman Hunt's picture 'The Light of the World', portraying Jesus standing outside a bramble-covered door. The door, we were told, represented our life, and the preacher pointed out that it had no handle on the outside. The message was not lost on me. In order for Jesus to come into my life I had to open the door to him

That moment came a few years later. By that time, with the support of my parents, I had combined membership of the choir with that of the local Crusader class (a non-denominational Bible-study group for boys). The class met on Sunday mornings before church service, so Sundays were busy days for me. Occasionally we had special social meetings, usually teas, at which a visiting speaker would challenge us directly to commit our lives to Christ. The outward sign that we had done this was to go up and shake hands with the speaker afterwards (how formal this all sounds nowadays!). On this occasion, I must have been moved and convinced by what was said, for I made that inner commitment and duly shook the proffered hand. I am sure that my grounding in the Church of England, lovingly nurtured by my parents, was a vital background to what happened, in addition to the teaching of the Crusader class.

I now see that this was certainly the most important decision of my life, yet it seemed oddly submerged in many other happenings. I was very busy at school with work, and at home with hobbies. Soon afterwards I won a scholarship which took me unexpectedly to a public school for the next four-and-a-half years as a boarder. Here, my new-found faith was not nurtured, despite confirmation and daily chapel – in fact, the latter was a daily duty enlivened only by the opportunity of singing in the choir. At that time, the school had no Christian Union or club where my faith could have developed freely (the situation has now improved). Eventually I consciously abandoned Christianity under the pressures of adolescence and boarding-school life. In most other ways, the debt I owe to the school is enormous, but it did not help me grow spiritually.

My faith did not flower again until I was a student at Cambridge, studying modern languages. By the end of the second year, I was morally, psychologically and spiritually confused, and I started desperately searching for God. I did not realise that he was already in me, for I had invited him in eight years before. I sensed him speaking to me, telling me – of all things – to go to the island of Patmos in Greece and read the gospel of John. In the long vacation of 1964 I found myself in the cave of the Revelation (then, as now, an Orthodox shrine) reading the gospel and praying. The light of God's truth flooded into me; looking back, I would say that

I was filled with the Holy Spirit. Jesus' words, 'I am the way, the truth and the life. No one comes to the father except through me'(John 14.6) convinced me fully, and I accepted him again without question as my Saviour and Lord. I remember walking across the island joyfully singing Stanford's B-flat setting of The Magnificat at the top of my voice, which must have surprised any Greek islander who happened to be listening.

I returned to Cambridge determined to put this rediscovered faith into practice. My friends were astonished, and to my sorrow and surprise many of them dropped me like a hot potato. I was probably threatening in my zeal, certainly at times rather priggish. I did not, however, join the (evangelical) Christian Union in the college. If it existed, I was unaware of it. I started to attend chapel regularly, and otherwise recited Matins and Evensong alone in my room. I also explored the possibility of ordination into the Anglican ministry, feeling that my commitment to Christ should be expressed through becoming a priest

Surprisingly, I was accepted as an ordination candidate first time round (the selectors nowadays would require much more experience of life). Immediately after graduating from Cambridge, I started to train for the ministry of the Church of England. I did not, however, go to an English theological college, but took the unusual step of training in Edinburgh at the Scottish Episcopal College, and combining my training there with the B.D. (Batchelor of Divinity) degree course at New College, the Divinity Faculty of Edinburgh University.

It was in Edinburgh that my ecclesiastical horizons began to widen. The experience of Scottish Presbyterianism was entirely new but very welcome. My teachers included a galaxy of rich and varied characters, mostly scholars of distinction. I remember being astonished when Professor Tom Torrance led college prayers by reciting the Te Deum (which I had thought was reserved for Anglicans). I enjoyed hearing the fine preaching of James Stewart (then Professor of New Testament), and listening to the visionary ideas of Lord MacLeod, founder of the Iona Community, down from the island on one of his regular visits. I realised that here were Christians with a different background and heritage to my own, but one as authentic and worthy of respect. I could not understand the narrow-minded attitude of some of my Anglican brethren, who saw Presbyterian ministries and sacraments as somehow 'invalid' (I had no qualms at all about receiving communion at the New College service). Since then, I have never had difficulty accepting and having fellowship with Christians of other theological or denominational backgrounds, once I have got to know them and sensed the genuineness of their commitment to Christ.

After three years in Edinburgh, which included a term as an exchange student at the Lutheran divinity faculty of Tübingen University in West Germany, I won a scholarship which enabled me to spend a year at Harvard Divinity School in the USA doing a Th. M. (Master of Theology) degree in New Testament studies. By this time I was wide open to any form of Christianity that I could take on board – too open. My thinking about the Bible and my theological perspectives were becoming muddled as I ploughed further into the more sceptical and rarified reaches of 'liberal' New Testament scholarship. It was with relief that I returned to England to become ordained (in Canterbury Cathedral, by Archbishop Michael Ramsey) and started work as a curate in Kent.

It was here that the deepest changes of my life and character started to happen, changes that have been going on ever since. I was at that time (1970) a liberal intellectual with little grasp of how most people tick, and with a very privileged background. I had a desire to serve God and to help people but no clear idea of how to do this. As curate, I was plunged into a mundane round of activities. One of these was youth work, for which I was ill-prepared. I ran (or attempted to run!) an 'open' youth club in the church hall, and also led a small discussion group of the more 'committed' (i.e. confirmed) teenagers

I soon realised certain things that made me take a long, hard look at myself. Some of the teenagers in the youth club had enormous needs, including drug problems. I was actually involved as a Crown witness in a case involving illegal receipt of herein by a member of the club. Much of the theology that I had imbibed, particularly at Harvard, left me quite unprepared to help these lads. Equally, I lacked the conviction really to lead the church's young people into a living relationship with Jesus. This was partly because I had never been trained in personal evangelism, and partly because my own relationship with the Lord was at a very low ebb, encrusted as it was with layers of sceptical theology. It was then that it began to dawn on me that the only Christians in the town who really know how to handle young people effectively were the evangelicals.

At first I found this hard to accept. I had encountered evangelicals before, for example at New College. My perspective on them was moulded by our family background. I had an evangelical great-aunt who, though loving and saintly, was also extremely narrow-minded. So I grew up thinking of evangelicals as people with a shocked reaction to the theatre (and even to novels, because they were 'not real'), rigid views about dress and the Sabbath, and a deep distrust of Roman Catholicism (usually referred to as 'Popery'). My own upbringing, for which I am profoundly grateful to my parents, positively encouraged me to participate in drama and music, and to appreciate the creative arts and literature. I was taken to the theatre and concerts from an early age, and our home housed a collection of hundreds of books which I was able to dip into at leisure.

Given this background, plus my theological sophistication, it was understandable that I should distrust evangelicals as naïve, dogmatic and intellectually dishonest. I had pigeon-holed the very positive experience of Crusaders as something suitable for 12-year-olds which was no longer relevant. Nor did I then realise how much the evangelical outlook had changed since my great-aunt's heyday. I could not, however, deny their effectiveness in attracting young people to their churches. The Free Evangelical and Brethren churches locally seemed to be bursting to the seams with them. I remember being invited to an evangelistic barbecue put on, I think, by the Brethren in the grounds of a large house. There were literally dozens of teenagers roaming around. I was impressed by the number, but mystified as to what had drawn them to the event. When I heard the speaker, I was even more astonished. He majored on Hell, a subject which I myself would have avoided like the plague on such an occasion. What amazed me was that he held the attention of his young audience when I would have expected them to have been put off. What was it about evangelicals that enabled them to attract these teenagers? It was galling to realise that my more 'enlightened' approach didn't seem to be leading them to God nearly as effectively.

Other evangelical influences began to impinge upon me. A very traditional, elderly member of our congregation unexpectedly lent me *God's Smuggler* by Brother Andrew.[1] This account of God's miraculous dealings intrigued me. Till then, I had no idea that Bibles were being smuggled behind the Iron Curtain, still less that miracles accompanied the smuggling. Then a girl who had left our church to join the Pentecostals lent me a copy of *'Renewal'* magazine[2] and the book *The Spirit Bade Me Go* by David du Plessis.[3] Reading these, I became vividly aware of Pentecostalism in a new way. I realised that Pentecostal phenomena such as 'tongues' were occurring in the historic denominational churches. At the same time, I became painfully aware of my own spiritual dryness and emptiness. Then I read two articles by Michael Harper[4] (in, of all places, the *Church Times*) which really made me sit up. Here was an Anglican priest recounting his experience of these phenomena in the most 'establishment' Anglican weekly. Perhaps, after all, this movement of the spirit was something which could renew me personally without causing me to commit intellectual suicide and join the evangelicals.

It also attracted me because it seemed to be operating across all denominational divisions.

One evening, feeling particularly vulnerable and spiritually dry, I prayed to be baptised in the Holy Spirit, not really understanding what I was asking. I did not feel at all different after this. However, a few weeks later I found myself in a large gathering for worship at a conference on charismatic renewal. I had never before seen the Holy Spirit move upon a room full of worshippers. The dignified spontaneity, the prophecy, the vivid 'pictures' shared, and the singing in tongues were all profoundly impressive. Most striking of all, a woman broke down in tears. Immediately a supportive group gathered round, praying quietly, their arms around her. 'I've never seen anything like this in a church service before,' I thought. 'I don't know what's happening, but it's real and I've got to pursue it.'

By that time (1972) I had been offered, and accepted, the post of Chaplain of King's College, Cambridge, my own undergraduate college. The chaplain's role in King's was basically a pastoral one, looking after the needs of the students as part of a team including the deans, tutors, etc.. In addition to this, there were the daily services in the famous chapel, which involved the daunting task of singing the responses with the equally famous choir. As a college, King's in 1972 was a difficult mixture of left-wing rebellion and extreme traditionalism.

The commited Christians in the college were mainly members of the Christian Union – evangelicals of various shades of theological 'conservatism' from different denominational backgrounds. They were also the staunchest supporters of the chapel services. As chaplain, I felt it my duty to encourage them, and I went along to their meetings – much their initial alarm, I think! I was won over by their sheer niceness, their sincerity, and their thoughtful approach to life (and to the Bible). They were certainly not the naïve, narrow-minded stereotype of evangelicals that I had despised. I was particularly impressed by their sensitive care of the adult Down's

Syndrome son of an elderly widow who worked for the college. She was a Roman Catholic who had taken her son to Lourdes several times. This in no way deterred the CU group. They visited the son at home, organised parties for him in college, and even helped bath and care for him when his mother could not cope. Sadly, he eventually fell ill and died. They continued to support and encourage his mother, even after they had graduated and left Cambridge. This sort of practical Christianity made me value them even more as friends. Evangelicals were going up my estimation.

At the same time, my investigations into the charismatic renewal continued. I had heard that one of the main centres of this in Cambridge was St Matthew's Church. A few of King's students attended St Matthew's, and I went with them to a mid-week meeting in the vicarage. Every inch of the floor seemed to be occupied. Students and townsfolk, jam-packed together, mingled without any awkwardness. Once again, I sensed the powerful presence of the Holy Spirit. Young people spontaneously praised God in a way that I had never heard before. I saw a fervour, a commitment, and an openness to the supernatural. A few weeks later, at another meeting (this time in church), I was kneeling at the communion rail as the vicar, Sidney Sims, prayed for me for healing of a minor infection. As he finished I found myself asking, 'While you are here, would you please pray for me to be baptised in the Spirit? He laid his hands on my head and began praying in tongues. Inwardly I surrendered myself to God, and in faith opened my mouth to pray. An unknown language flooded out. I was filled with joy and released into praise. To my great surprise, my hands floated above my head, and I started praising God as I had never praised him before.

I arrived back in King's in a state of turmoil. Had I commited intellectual suicide? Something very extraordinary had certainly happened to me. Feverishly, I read everything I could lay my hands on about speaking in tongues, Pentecostalism and charismatic renewal. God started to churn things up in my spirit. Deep-rooted personal sins had to be confessed, and God's forgiveness received. My attitude to the Bible changed radically. I became much more open to accepting what it said literally, whereas before my training had led me to dissect it according to the historical-critical method. Far from being restricted by a more conservative attitude to Scripture, I have since found it enormously liberating. I have also found that I can use all the tools of biblical scholarship which I acquired at Edinburgh and Harvard while retaining a more conservative attitude to the text. It is encouraging that the number of well-respected conservative biblical scholars seems to be increasing.

The next three years at King's were a time of adjustment to a new phase in my life and ministry. After a period of repentance and emotional healing, God started to use me in all sorts of new ways. I was so enthused by a tape on inner healing lent me by a student that when the lady who cleaned my room started opening up to me about past hurts in her life I found myself praying for her. God clearly touched her, and she later told me that she was so peaceful after praying that she had slept for twelve hours the following night. I also became aware of more sinister supernatural forces. Together with a House Church leader and an elderly Brethren couple, I was involved in prayer for an undergraduate who asked for deliverance from evil spirits. A few weeks previously I would have pooh-poohed the idea of a personal devil. Now, the existence of Satan was only too real as the young man writhed on the floor, the demons in him reacting to the name of Jesus, verses of Scripture and the Apostles' Creed. Eventually he was completely freed, and I believe that he is now pastor of a thriving church.

In 1974 I heard Michael Harper speaking inspiringly about his experience of charismatic communities in the USA. I decided to go and see them for myself. I visited an interdenominational young people's community in Pennsylvania, and the Church of the Redeemer,

21

Houston, an Anglican church which at that time was organised in community households. There I saw God working at a deep level as men and women committed themselves to sharing their lives, homes and possessions in a radical way reminiscent of the early Jerusalem church. These communities were also experiencing and ministering healing, and many in the neighbourhood were being helped and indeed converted.

I returned determined to live in community myself. In 1975 the job at King's finished, and I joined the staff of St Matthew's as curate. I was to lead a small community in a house next to the church. Unfortunately this was not a success. We made every mistake in the book! We did not know each other well enough, nor did we share the same vision for the community. Considering the difficulties we encountered, it's amazing we all emerged relatively unscathed. Still, I had caught a glimpse of the church as a community of love and commitment, and have never lost this vision.

January 1977 saw the opening of a new chapter in my life. I moved to Bristol to be one of the Anglican chaplains to the university, and have been in Bristol ever since. My main responsibility was to look after the Monica Wills Memorial Chapel, a small building seating at most 120 people, which is part of the Wills Hall of residence. This chapel had by statute to be interdenominational. When I arrived it was being used as a base by a worshipping community of between eighty and a hundred students. My predecessor, Donald Werner, had built up a lively work among the students. Evangelical, charismatic, and well-qualified theologically, Don was convinced of the need to gather a core-group of students who were open both to the Word and the Spirit of God. Students responded to his clear teaching and uncompromising leadership. Many came to faith in Christ, and the chapel community grew from its original core of twelve.

I had already heard about this development in Bristol, so I was thrilled to be able to take over a job which so exactly suited my own experience and convictions. It perfectly combined student work with charismatic renewal and a basis of biblical teaching. It was also completely interdenominational. The congregation consisted of Anglicans, members of most Free Churches (including Pentecostals and House Churches), a few Roman Catholics, and some new converts with no other church background. An Anglican chaplain was in charge simply because the Anglican chaplaincy, with four chaplains, was the only one which could afford virtually to second a full-time worker to the chapel.

We had two Sunday services. The morning one was formal, consisting of hymns, prayers, readings, an address and Holy Communion. For those who were the committed core, plus interested and adventurous visitors, there was the much freer evening meeting, during which we shared spiritual gifts, including prophecies and tongues with interpretation. Every term there was a houseparty with a speaker (including such well-known renewal leaders as Colin Urquhart[5] and Michael Harper).

The existence of this community of young Christians was a wonderful work of God. If it lacked anything it was the stability of really open and committed relationships. After a year, I set up small cell-groups that met midweek. These had the desired effect. The commitment of chapel members to one another grew. Gradually, a few students who graduated got jobs in Bristol and continued to attend the chapel. They became in effect the building blocks of a fellowship that was to emerge.

The catalyst for this unusual development was a mere matter of money. By 1979 I had begun to feel dissatisfied with my work. I was fed up with the constant throughput of students (a university does rather resemble a sausage-machine!). I told the Bishop that I was thinking of making a move. Almost immediately I heard that if I left I would not be replaced. I tried to think of ways in which the chapel community could be pastored. It took six months for me to reach the inescapable conclusion that God wanted me to stay on, supported financially by the chapel community – if they were willing. I was most reluctant to do this. I did not want to be labelled a schismatic; indeed, I was committed to working for renewal within Anglicanism. But God made it clear to me that I had to put the pastoral needs of the fellowship before my own prejudices. It was as if God painted me into a corner to make me walk through a door that I would otherwise have ignored.

The decision was complicated by the fact that I chose this moment to get married! Two enormous changes at once could have given rise to major stress. It was a great help that my wife Val was entirely with me in the decision. She had a remarkably similar background to mine, having also been one of the Anglican university chaplains. Through all the challenging, and occasionally difficult, times which were to come as our new church was established, she has been a tremendous encouragement and help to me.

Immediately after returning from our honeymoon I wrote to the then Bishop of Bristol informing him of my plans. He was kind, but nonplussed. He could not formally license me to a non-Anglican job (he later gave me his permission to officiate in Anglican churches in the diocese, which I was very happy to be able to do, and this has been extended by the present Bishop). So on 1st January, 1981, I became an Anglican priest working as a non-denominational Free Church pastor, supported financially by my own congregation. I also continued as a university chaplain, becoming, thanks to the support and approval of most of my chaplaincy colleagues, the 'non-denominational' chaplain to the university.

What has happened since then provides the immediate background to this book. Our fellowship, renamed 'Fellowship of the King', moved its meetings to the university Students' Union. We now meet in a hired Anglican church building for our main evening meeting. Numbers have gradually increased, and over the years both the composition and the vision of our church have enlarged. We now have roots in the city of Bristol. Of

250 adult members, only thirty are students. Though perhaps three-quarters are university graduates, a significant and growing proportion are not. The majority of our members are aged between eighteen and thirty and there are forty children, most aged three and under. This makes us an unusual church, and the lack of older and more experienced Christians can result in a certain imbalance. On the other hand, there is plenty of zeal and commitment, and I am constantly amazed at the maturity of our young leadership. We are learning how to train new leaders to cope with the numerical growth which we feel will come, and which is surely God's plan for his Church as a whole.

Our main meetings are all held in hired premises. The one building owned by the church is a four-storey house in Clifton, quite near the university. This contains the church office and a common room, and houses the library. It is also the home of a small community of committed church members who have a ministry of hospitality. We have four full-time church workers: two pastors, an administrator and an evangelist/teacher/musician. We also support an ophthalmologist and his family whom we have sent out to Tanzania, and partly support a number of other missionaries and ministries outside the fellowship.

Our development has not been a smooth success-story, however. We have had to learn through our mistakes. The unity within our own church has occasionally been put under considerable strain. We are learning hard lessons about our personal walk with God, repentance, forgiveness, and commitment to one another.

We are also involved as a church in various inter-church activities within Bristol. Some are evangelistic, others express social concern, others involve prophetic teaching, others prayer and worship. All are valuable bridge-building exercises expressing something of the unity of the church in the city. Such activities are of vital importance as we move towards that unity which is God's heart for the church.

My concern for unity, then, arises from the way that God has led me. It is practical as well as theoretical, and is still being worked out. This book will be out-of-date by the time it is published, because God is continually moving his church on, writing new chapters in our experience and understanding.

PART II

God's Blueprint for Unity

Chapter 3

Back to Basics

One big problem about approaching church unity is that we tend to think immediately about unity *between* churches. The New Testament writers, however, don't approach unity in that way. They concentrate on unity *within* churches. Our consideration of unity tends to centre on structures, theology and joint activity; the Bible centres on relationships within the body of Christ. It might therefore be helpful if we narrowed down our focus to the local church situation. But before even looking at relationships between Christians, we need to consider our relationship with God. There are two dimensions to this.

The first is *new birth* (i.e. spiritual birth). It seems almost too obvious to state, but in order to enjoy Christian unity, we need to be Christian. I was brought up in an Anglicanism that did not care to distinguish too closely between the saved and the unsaved. I am aware that a very large number of church people are attracted to 'universalism', i.e. the belief that everyone will be saved in the end, whether they have faith in Jesus Christ or not. I was myself a universalist before God made it very plain to me through reading and meditating on the Scriptures that this was an impossible position to square with the plain sense of the text. For example, Jesus' words to Nicodemus in John's gospel chapter 3, verse 3, are clear enough: 'I tell you the truth, no one can see the kingdom of God unless he is born again'.

The word 'again' can be translated 'from above'; either way, it points to the activity of the Holy Spirit in a person's life, as Jesus explains in John chapter 3, verse 5: 'I tell you the truth, no one can enter the kingdom of God unless he is born of water and the spirit.' 'Water' to Nicodemus would have suggested John the Baptist's baptism of repentance.[1] The fresh element in Jesus' teaching was the vital role of the Holy Spirit in this new birth. Jesus goes on to make it plain that only the Holy Spirit can give life to the spirit of man: 'flesh gives birth to flesh, but the Spirit gives birth to spirit' (John 3.6).

There is a two-fold dimension to that new spiritual birth. On the one hand, there is *what God has done in Christ*. Peter writes, 'He (Christ) himself bore our sins in his body on the tree, so that we might die to sins and live for righteousness; by his wounds you have been healed' (I Peter 2.24). Jesus died for us. He bore our sins, and the penalty for them, death. The New Testament is crystal clear about this. It is God's act on our behalf. The second dimension is *our response*, which should be one of *repentance, faith and commitment*. To be drawn into God's purpose of redemption, we need to accept the lordship of Jesus Christ, entering his kingdom, i.e. putting ourselves under his authority. In doing this, we allow the Holy Spirit to take up residence in our spirit and bring about the new birth. Peter too writes of this new birth, linking it with the Resurrection and the future hope of our place in heaven: 'in his (God's) great mercy he has given us new birth into a living hope through the Resurrection of Jesus Christ from the dead' (I Peter 1.3).

In speaking of the meaning of our salvation, the New Testament uses a rich variety of symbols and illustrations, e.g. Old Testament temple sacrifice, the freeing of slaves, the exodus from Egypt, legal judgment, adoption into sonship, and many others. The picture of new birth is only one of these, but it is a particularly vivid one which goes back to Jesus himself. It describes the radical difference between a non-Christian and a Christian. Paul speaks to Christians as 'dead in your sins' (Eph. 2.1) before their conversion, but then as 'made alive with Christ' (v.5). He also speaks of conversion as moving from darkness into light (I Peter 2.9).

A Christian, then, is someone who has made a complete break with the past. He has turned from his old sinful life and put his faith in Jesus Christ who, he believes, died for him on the cross, taking his sins upon himself. He has been changed and indeed continues to be changed, by the Holy Spirit working within him. He is caught up into a relationship with God which is one of unity: unity of heart and mind, spirit and purposes. So, for example, Paul says that 'God has poured out his love into our hearts by the Holy Spirit, who he has given us'. And in I Corinthians chapter 2, verse 16, he affirms, 'We have the *mind* of Christ'. The relationship between the believer and the Lord is to be so close that our own sinful self is totally eclipsed by the overwhelming presence and holiness of Christ indwelling us through his spirit. So Paul can write, 'I have been crucified with Christ, and I no longer live, but Christ lives in me. The life I live in the body, I live by faith in the Son of God, who loved me and gave himself for me' (Gal. 2.20).

This new, spiritual birth, and the subsequent ongoing daily relationship with Christ by faith, is what marks a Christian. To my mind, the new birth does not have to be experienced on one clear occasion which can be precisely timed and dated. Many do indeed have such an experience, either alone, or at a service of worship or, often, at an evangelistic meeting. But, as a pastor, I am aware of many Christians who have passed gradually into the reality of the Christian life. They may have been aware of Christ in their lives guiding and loving them as far back as they can remember, and their commitment deepened and matured as they grew. Or they experienced, perhaps, a period of months during which interest developed into commitment with no particular milestones to mark the transition. It does not seem to matter very much how it happens. The important thing, surely, is that it *does* happen. The proof that it has happened is that it then continues. John writes, 'Our fellowship is with the Father and with his Son, Jesus Christ' (I John 1.3). An ongoing relationship with the living God is surely the most important and wonderful relationship a human being can have.

Part of the difficulty in achieving unity between Christians has, I think, to do with this basic commitment and ongoing relationship. It may well be that not all the members of a church are Christians. I have heard more than one evangelist say that going to church does not make you a Christian any more than going to a garage makes you a car. This may seem trite but it's true. It is possible to be friendly with non-Christians, to love and be loved by them, and to exchange hospitality and all sorts of kindnesses with them. What is not possible is to share with them that *spiritual* unity of heart and mind.

If the non-Christians are church members, there is real confusion. No possibility of spiritual unity within any congregation will exist until the non-Christians are converted. This is a surprisingly common situation.

Many vicars and ministers, on moving to a new church, have to start their evangelism among their own congregation.[2] A similar difficulty occurs when some Christians in a local church have become lukewarm in their commitment to Christ. In that case, they are often held in the church by the network of friendly social relationships that they have established. But because true Christian unity depends at root on each individual's relationship with God, these relationships within the church become superficial, unreal, and increasingly strained. The only way to resolve the problem is for the lukewarm Christian to seek God again with fresh zeal, working through whatever problems may have led to the falling-away with a loving and understanding Christian pastor, friend or counsellor.

The ongoing daily basis of a Christian's 'vertical' unity with God is *prayer*. Prayer continually reminds us of the reality of our fellowship with God. It is also the basis of 'horizontal' unity within the local church, and beyond. Prayer involves both talking to God and listening to what he has to say to us through the Bible and the Holy Spirit.

To maintain a regular habit of daily prayer, it is important to establish a disciplined routine. In his book *Ordering your Private World*, Gordon MacDonald emphasises the need to programme prayer into our timetable.[3] If we don't, it will be crowded out. At least half of our difficulty with praying would be solved if we planned it, giving God the priority that he deserves. On our main annual family holiday, when we aim to get right away and be alone with the children, Val and I take time in the evenings to discuss this aspect of our lives. Are we setting each other free to spend time with the Lord? We examine the way we organise each day, and try to be as honest as possible with each other. I believe that each individual and married couple needs regularly to assess the place of prayer in their lives.

At the same time as making sure that we actually do give time to prayer, we need to make the best of our time with God, which is as precious to him as it is to us. First of all, we are coming to a God who is our loving heavenly Father. This fundamental truth is expressed at the beginning of the Lord's Prayer in the simple words, 'Our Father'. No other world religion teaches this intimate way of addressing God. Christians can address God as Father because through Jesus' death and Resurrection we have been adopted into his family. We need to reassert this relationship of sonship every day, thus expressing the unity we have with the Father through Christ, in the Holy Spirit.

Spiritually, the most difficult period of my life was a time of about six months during 1984 when I mysteriously lost any sense of assurance that God loved me, that he had saved me and would save me. I now know that he allowed me to go through that experience of desolation in order to strengthen some shaky foundation stones of my commitment to Christ. In my need, I allowed myself to be vulnerable to Christian friends, whose love and prayers were invaluable, and I found myself driven back to God in prayer.

I vividly remember the moment of dramatic breakthrough into a new and solid realisation of God's love for me. I was at a conference of Christian leaders, and we had just heard an eye-witness report about revival in South Africa. The speaker concluded by asking God to release the power and love of the Holy Spirit upon the meeting. As she prayed, I felt compelled to prostrate myself on the floor. When I did so, I started to sob –

33

deep sobs welling up from within – and found myself repeating 'Father, Father, Father'. From that moment, I began to have a new awareness of God's love for me, and the Scriptures that speak of that love started to hit me in a way that I hadn't known before. Since then, my prayer times have increasingly been intimate meetings between me and a Father who loves me, cares for me, understands me through and through, and will never let me go. I don't have to earn his approval – he just loves me. The objective and convincing proof of this is that he sent his Son to die for me. I also see daily signs of his love in a thousand different ways – including things that some people would consider too trivial to mention. But isn't it reassuring to know that God is so big that he even cares about whether or not his children can find a parking-space?

John, the beloved disciple, had no doubts about a Christian's relationship with God when he wrote, 'Our fellowship is with the Father and with his Son, Jesus Christ' (I John 1.3). It is our privilege to come into God's presence as those who have rights and a relationship as his children. The first and most appropriate way we can express this fact is to tell God how much we love him. Occasionally, our children actually say that to us (sometimes they even write little notes to us saying so), and it really gladdens our hearts. The way we tell God is through *worship*. It includes thanksgiving, praise and adoration. As we 'hallow God's name', blessing and praising him, we open ourselves to God's love for us. Just as we, as human parents, appreciate it when our children tell us that they love us, so God's heart warms as he hears us express our love for him, and he pours his love into us.

More and more, worship and praise are becoming part of my own prayer life. How can we worship God in church on Sundays if we are not regularly praising him on weekdays? We *need* to show our love to him in this way. I usually express my worship by singing. Many new worship songs are simply addressing God directly, and can helpfully be used in our own times of prayer.

Incidentally, God is not bothered if we sing flat, or out of time. If we follow Jesus' advice to go into a room apart and close the door, we won't embarrass ourselves or anyone else, and we certainly won't embarrass God. He is delighted with any offering of love and praise that we bring, just as human parents are thrilled with their child's performance of a simple piano piece (despite one or two wrong notes).

In some ways, the most exciting part of prayer is allowing God to speak to us. The essential tool for this is a copy of the Bible, although God does use other ways of speaking (a friend of mine was once addressed by God through some words written on the side of a truck that he spied out of a train window!). Basically, God wants us to soak up the words of Scripture so that they become part of our very being. To do that, it is helpful if we can read large chunks *and* meditate on small chunks. By 'meditation' I do not mean some mystical exercise, or intellectual study. I simply want to hear God speaking to me through the words. At the moment, I am meditating on Mark's gospel, section by section. I first ask God to speak to me through what I am about to read. I then read the passage, and think about it, allowing my thoughts to be guided by the Holy Spirit. Then I respond to what he says by expressing my thoughts in prayer. I usually pray out loud, as it makes prayer more real and concrete.

Today, for example, I meditated briefly on the short paragraph in which Jesus predicts Peter's denial (Mark 14.27–31). I felt that God was challenging me about keeping my word, and about being courageous when my faith is under attack. I responded by asking God to help me in these areas, and by thanking him for his love in forgiving me just as he forgave Peter.

I find this approach to the Bible so helpful that I never now use Bible-reading notes, though I encourage church members to use notes if they find them helpful. It is amazing how God uses my readings to challenge, encourage and guide me.

When Jesus taught his disciples to pray 'Give us this

day our daily bread', I don't think that he was referring simply to our material needs. He declared, 'I am the bread of life. He who comes to me will never go hungry, and he who believes in me will never be thirsty' (John 6.35). At the deepest level, the 'daily bread' we pray for is surely Jesus himself. In order to feed on him, our staple diet has to be the Bible, his word to us, which the Holy Spirit makes alive and relevant to our personal situation.

Christian unity, then, begins and ends with our relationship with God. Inseparably linked with that is *our relationship with other Christians*. One of the reasons that Christ died was that his disciples should be truly united in him. The apostle John sees this clearly when he comments on Caiaphas' words that Jesus would die for the people: 'He did not say this on his own, but as high priest that year he prophesied that Jesus would die for the Jewish nation, and not only for that nation but also for the scattered children of God, to bring them together and make them one' (John 11.51–2). John also closely links Christ's death with the unity of Christians when he meditates on the love of God in his first epistle: 'This is love: not that we loved God, but that he loved us and sent his Son as an atoning sacrifice for our sins. Dear friends, since God so loved us, we ought also to love one another' (I John 4.10–11).

Paul too sees the unity of the church as one of the purposes of Christ's death, and a direct result of it. He writes warmly of Christ on the cross breaking down the greatest social and religious barrier for a devout first century Jew, that between Jew and Gentile: 'His purpose was to create in himself one new man out of the two, thus making peace, and in this one body to reconcile both of them to God through the cross, by which he put to death their hostility' (Eph. 2.15–6). The 'body' referred to here is clearly the church, 'God's new society' (to borrow the title of John Stott's commentary on Ephesians), the only social grouping where unity in Christ can be worked out and expressed. Finally, in Galatians chapter 3, verse 26, Paul portrays faith in Christ as the greatest unifying force in society, again seeing the church as the one social structure where all man-made divisions are (potentially) abolished: 'There is neither Jew nor Greek, slave nor free, male nor female, for you are all one in Christ Jesus'. Stott comments, 'The new society God has brought into being is nothing short of a new creation, a new human race, whose characteristic is no longer alienation but reconciliation, no longer division and hostility but unity and peace.'[4]

The outstanding feature of this new society is *God's love in action*. The 'new commandment' given by Jesus to his disciples the night before he was crucified was to love one another as he had loved them (John 13.34). Because Jesus died on the cross, this has become possible for all his followers. As he has loved and forgiven us, so we can love and forgive one another. As he has reconciled us to the Father, so he has given us the ministry of reconciliation (II Cor. 5.18).

Unfortunately, this does not happen easily or automatically. Jesus has won for us the possibility of true unity, but we have to pray and work single-mindedly to make it real. We have to face constant daily temptations to be disunited. Over the last twenty-five years, I have made the momentous discovery that Christians are not perfect! The problem is that often I saddle them with my unreasonable expectations. Usually, it must be said, my brothers and sisters in Christ are warm in their love, generous in their appreciation, welcoming, positive, and clearly showing the influence of Christ on their lives. Occasionally, however, they are not, and I get hurt and upset.

All of us will have experienced this from time to time. Often, paradoxically, it is the very fact of getting closer to another Christian that leads to disillusionment. We so want to express our love for one another, so we become more open, and therefore vulnerable and easily hurt. We begin to see people as they really are. Whereas in a marriage relationship we are helped to work through the difficulties by knowing that we are doing so on the basis of a life commitment, in other relationships in the church we can so easily retreat and not bother.

If we want to take Christian unity seriously, however, we *have* to bother. The first thing that we must do is to keep short accounts with God about any wrong attitudes, remarks or actions with respect to another Christian. Small personality differences can assume enormous proportions. Whenever we are working together as a team, Satan tries to get in and cause division. I have experienced this in our leadership team from time to time. We are all very different personalities. We have the potential to rub up against one another. When we are acting selfishly, trying to push our own point of view and pressurise one another, our team meetings are agony.

On the other hand, when we lovingly submit to one another, listening carefully and making allowances for one another's character and weaknesses, we find that we complement each other. God has put us together for a purpose. We discover that he has chosen us carefully, because he wants to build a strong team. But we must make it our priority to seek his will together, taking our goals from him and coming to decisions that are reached in an atmosphere of mutual commitment and prayer.

In all this, there is a world of difference between a negative and a positive attitude to our Christian co-workers. If we view one another critically, we immediately allow Satan free access into the relationship. On the other hand, if we try to see the best in one another, discerning each other's potential in Christ and encouraging one another as much as possible, God is able to use our complementary gifts to strengthen one another.

It is important to realise this in churches where close and potentially fruitful relationships are developing within the structures. It might be, for example, that home groups have been going for a few years and are just beginning to achieve something. People are beginning to love and care for one another in a new way, there is a desire to go out and evangelise, and members are starting to pray enthusiastically for the sick. It is precisely in that sort of situation that niggles develop. When they do, *we must not retreat*. Satan is trying to stop us from entering into the good things that God has for us. We must press on and get through the difficulties.

How do we do this? Basically, we need to use two great gifts that God has given Christians: *confession* and *forgiveness*. First, *confession*. As Christians, we are forgiven sinners. It is possible for us not to sin – 'Sin shall not be your master, because you are not under law, but under grace' (Roman 6.14). Yet our old nature (what St Paul calls 'the flesh') keeps reasserting itself, and we do still sin. Sin separates us from God, and mars our unity both with him and with other Christians. So what should we do about our sin?

The Bible gives a clear answer: confess it to God. 'If we confess our sins', St John writes, 'he is faithful and just and will forgive us our sins and purify us from all unrighteousness' (I John 1.9). God's forgiveness is immediate and total. It is based on Jesus' death for us. The blood Jesus shed on the cross is, as it were, applied to our sin now. 'The blood of Jesus, his Son, purifies us from all sin' (v.7).

Each day in my time of prayer I ask God to bring into my mind sins that I have commited which I need to confess. Usually these sins fall into familiar categories, which include the wrong thoughts and feelings I have had about other Christians. The process of confession is a humbling one. I say I am sorry, ask for forgiveness, ask that I may be strengthened in that weak area, and then receive God's forgiveness. Each time that I do this wholeheartedly and honestly, I believe that God is able to deal, at a deep level, with the origins of my sin. I know that he is changing me for the better, because he is reshaping me in the likeness of his Son. This process takes a long time, unfortunately!

Forgiveness is the God-given way for me to deal with sin that has been committed against me. Because of Jesus' death on the cross for me, I am able to forgive even my enemies (let alone other Christians). Since God has forgiven them, I am in no position to withhold my forgiveness. This was Jesus' clear teaching. He told Peter that sins should be forgiven seventy-seven times (Matt. 18.22), by which he meant 'totally' – seven represents completeness in the numerical symbolism of the Bible. He then told the story of the unforgiving servant to show how angry God is with us if we do not forgive our brother from the heart (v.35). God requires us to forgive those who have hurt and persecuted us. If we do not, he warns us that we will be held under his judgment (v.34), and that we ourselves will not be able to receive his forgiveness (Matt. 6.15).

In our prayers, we need to be very rigorous with ourselves, and ask God to show us whether there are people who have hurt us whom we haven't forgiven. I know that I can think that I am clear of unforgiveness, but then unconsciously give myself away by the way I talk about people. We may often have to ask God to forgive us for harbouring bitterness and resentment against people for the hurt that they have caused us. Such hurt may be very real, and our bitterness very human and understandable. Nevertheless, God's standards are rigorous. He expects his people to be no less forgiving than he is. It is significant that the word used for 'sin' is in fact 'debt'. In the same way that a kindly creditor might release a debtor from his debt, so God wants us to 'release' from our negative hostile thoughts and emotions those who have sinned against us. Note that we usually do this on our own, in God's presence. Often it doesn't help to go to a person and say, 'You have hurt me, but I forgive you' – particularly if they are unaware that they have done so.

Sometimes, however, our prayer to be forgiven and to forgive may have to be followed by action. Jesus gives clear instructions about two situations where this might be appropriate. First, if a Christian ('your brother') sins against you (Matt. 18.15–17), Jesus teaches that it may be necessary to go and talk to him about it. This would presumably be either because of your weakness – because you feel a need to talk to him about it and 'get things straight' – or because you feel that it needs to be discussed for his good. If you really have forgiven the person beforehand, the discussion will proceed in love as far as you are concerned, and you will be able to be loving even if the other person responds sharply to what you are saying.

The object of the exercise is for there to be reconciliation between you, so it is important to proceed in the right spirit. A critical, self-righteous approach won't be at all fruitful. You want to make it as easy as possible for the other person to see their fault and say 'sorry', and in the process, you may find that you, too, are apologising. In these sort of situations in the church, there are often faults on both sides. I occasionally say to our church that it is worth saying sorry even if you are 99 per cent in the right, just for that 1 per cent where you are in the wrong. In fact, your initial apology will often release the genuine love and repentance that is bottled up inside the person who has wronged you.

The next step recommended by Jesus (v.16) should only be taken if your initial approach fails. You must be sure that you have done everything in your power to win the other person over. But if they stubbornly refuse to listen to you, Jesus recommends that you go back with one or two fellow Christians. In a loving and prayerful discussion which is not too confrontational, reconciliation can usually be achieved.

The third step (v.17) should only be necessary on very rare occasions. A personal dispute ought never to be blown up into such proportions that the whole church is involved. This step is an absolute last resort, to be taken with extreme care. The other person would have to be very much in the wrong, be behaving in a bad spirit, and be reacting badly to the most loving discipline in a way that is affecting the whole church. I am glad to say that we have never had to go to such lengths in our church. But the fact that Jesus taught about such a situation proves that it could occur. Only after this final step had failed would a person be asked to leave a church.

The aim of this procedure is clearly reconciliation between two Christians. Jesus wants love and forgiveness

41

to prevail in his church. But for this to happen, we have to be real with one another. Christians often seem to me to divide into two groups: those who try to avoid conflict and confrontation at all costs, and those who self-righteously and insensitively try to engineer it. By contrast, the way of Jesus is the way of loving realism – of wooing the offender back to repentance and to God. Paul puts it very well: 'Brothers, if someone is caught in sin, you who are spiritual should restore him gently. But watch yourself, or you also may be tempted. Carry each others' burdens, and in this way you will fulfil the law of Christ' (Gal. 6.1–2).

Jesus teaches about a second situation, that of knowing that another Christian has something against you (Matt. 6.23–4). Jesus puts this situation in his own contemporary context of offering a sacrifice in the temple. Go and be reconciled before offering the sacrifice, he teaches. In our own context, this means that we cannot in all conscience praise God at a church service if we are aware that another Christian has something against us. We need to go to that person, ask them if there is anything the matter, listen with an open heart, and say sorry if necessary. In that way, the relationship should be restored.

I have gone into the question of forgiveness at some length because I am convinced it is one of the main keys to unity, both within the local church and between churches. I know just how easy it is for Christians to bear grudges against each other. What the writer to the Hebrews calls a 'bitter root' can so easily grow up in our life if we let it (Heb. 12.15). The writer goes on to say that this will 'cause trouble and defile many'. How right he is! The whole church is bound to be subtly affected by disagreements and bad feeling. People will take sides. What is more, bitter people will also harm themselves. Locked up in unforgiveness, they will 'miss the grace of God' (v.15). Much better to follow Jesus' good instructions to forgive (or lovingly confront) and be reconciled as soon as the wrong is done.

At the start of this chapter, I stated that I wanted to

concentrate on unity *within* churches – our personal relationships with God and with other Christians. In fact, this does turn out to be relevant to relationships *between* churches, and I want to end with a personal experience to prove it.

A few years ago, my wife and I were feeling very sore and hurt about the way we and our church had been treated by another church. We did not realise it fully at the time, but our feelings were festering away below the surface. Matters came to a head at a conference in London. I remember looking down from the gallery of the large auditorium and seeing the leaders of this particular church all sitting in a row in the stalls. Immediately all the negative feelings I had about them – hurt, bitterness, jealousy, and other unpleasant emotions – flooded over me. I knew then that I had to do something about it.

On returning home, I told my wife, and we decided to set aside an evening for getting right with God on this particular matter. First, we separately wrote down all the incidents we could remember when we had been hurt by the leaders or members of this particular church. Then, after comparing notes, we systematically forgave them for each incident. This required an act of the will, and it wasn't a great emotional experience. Finally, we asked God's forgiveness for the wrong feelings we had harboured against our brothers and sisters in Christ. The process took a whole evening, but we went to bed in peace knowing that we had obeyed God's command to love and forgive.

Soon afterwards, the genuineness of our forgiveness was tasted to the full. Mutual friends invited the leader of this church and his wife to spend the evening with us. Part of the reason for this was to achieve a reconciliation. In the course of the evening, I was able to ask the leader's forgiveness for our wrong attitudes. He responded by apologising for any way in which he or his church had hurt us. In this way, a wonderful reconciliation was achieved. We are now firm friends again, and our churches are increasingly co-operating in various projects in the city.

I mention this example to show that confession and forgiveness do work in bringing reconciliation between Christians. I urge any reader who is in a similar situation, either within your own church or between churches, to put these biblical principles into practice. You will be amazed at the results.

Commitment to God, prayer, love, forgiveness – these are the building blocks of Christian unity. But is there an outstanding example in history of a church where all these features were present and functioning correctly?

Chapter 4

As the Maker Intended

Whenever I look for God's blueprint for a united church, I am irresistibly drawn back to the original Jerusalem believers. J.B. Phillips describes his reaction to the book of Acts in the preface to his vivid translation of it: 'No one can read this book without being convinced that there is Someone here at work besides mere human beings. Perhaps because of their very simplicity, perhaps because of their readiness to believe, to obey, to give, to suffer, and if need be to die, the Spirit of God found what surely he must always be seeking – a fellowship of men and women so united in love and faith that he can work in them and through them with the minimum of let or hindrance.'[1]

We shall start our search by looking at some of the features of that church described in Acts chapters 2 to 6. These will serve as pointers to the sort of changes we should expect in our own church situations if we are to experience authentic unity of heart and soul.

The Jerusalem church began with the mighty event of Pentecost. It is true that few, if any, other churches have had such a dramatic start. But for a church to be truly united, both vertically with God and horizontally within itself, it has to start and to move on in the *dynamic power of the Holy Spirit*. In his address to the crowd, Peter saw this event as a fulfilment of Joel's prophecy of the outpouring of the Spirit in the last days and he describes Jesus as 'a man accredited by God to you by miracles, wonders and signs'. In other words, the miraculous aspect in Jesus' ministry and in the starting of the church was absolutely vital.

During these first few chapters of Acts, and indeed throughout the New Testament, miracles are crucial. The whole of Chapter 3 is devoted to the healing of the lame man, and this event gives rise to phenomenal church growth (2,000 new converts) and persecution

(Acts 4.5–Acts 8.22). Acts chapter 5, verses 12 to 16, also gives examples of apostolic signs and wonders resulting in continued growth and extraordinary scenes of healing in the streets.

A truly united church in our own day will, I believe, be likewise one which has been brought into being and is being moved on by the power of the Holy Spirit. There must be a supernatural dimension, otherwise we will not be one in God (John 17.21) but only through human friendship.[2]

The Jerusalem church was from the start *evangelistic*. It was brought into being by the power of the Holy Spirit and the preaching of the Gospel. In his address to the crowd at Pentecost (Acts 2.14–36), Peter speaks of Jesus: his life (v.22), his death (v.23), his resurrection (vv.24 and 32) and his ascension and giving of the Spirit (v.33). He then issues a clear evangelistic appeal: 'Repent and be baptised, every one of you, in the name of Jesus Christ for the forgiveness of your sins. And you will receive the gift of the Holy Spirit'. He continues with words that are oddly reminiscent of Jesus' prayer in John Chapter 17, verse 20, for those who will believe in him through the disciples' message: 'The promise is for you and your children and for all who are far off – for all whom the Lord our God will call.' Notice that this evangelistic appeal includes baptism and the gift of the Holy Spirit as well as repentance and forgiveness. There are no half-measures with Peter!

Throughout these chapters, the apostles continue to testify to the good news of the death and the Resurrection of Jesus. Whenever a crowd gathers, they preach (Acts 3.12–26); whenever they are challenged by the authorities, they preach (Acts 4.8–20; Acts 5.29–32), powerfully, and with enormous courage. After being flogged, and ordered not to continue their preaching, they ignore the order. 'Day after day, in the temple courts and from house to house, they never stopped teaching and proclaiming the good news that Jesus is the Christ' (Acts 5.42).

A united church will have a strong evangelistic

fervour. It will not be introverted, but committed to the service of the Lord who commissioned his disciples, 'Go and make disciples of all nations' (Matt. 28.20). God uses inter-church evangelism to unite churches in surprising and exciting ways, because when they join to preach the Gospel, they are functioning as the Maker intended.

The new Christians in Jerusalem had only the Old Testament. To understand how it pointed to Jesus as the Messiah, they had to have it expounded to them by the apostles. Peter's address in Acts chapter 2 is partly teaching, interpreting the Old Testament in the light of Jesus. The converts needed ongoing teaching to ground them throughly in the new 'Way', as the faith was first called (Acts 9.2).

Any truly united church has to be based similarly on the *apostolic teaching*, mediated for us through the Scriptures. This raises a number of problems. First, there is the question of the very authority of Scripture, subject as it now is to highly critical analysis by many scholars. Many Christians are confused as to what they should or should not believe in the light of science and modern scholarship. And even for those who do fully accept the authority of Scripture, there is the problem of how to interpret it. A particularly difficult passage may be interpreted in many different ways.

However, the Jerusalem Christians did not seem to share our problems either with the authority of Scripture or with its interpretation. They seem to have accepted the apostolic teaching without a murmur of criticism. I suggest that this was because the power of the Holy Spirit was so clearly present in the church, and the connection between this and the death and the Resurrection of Jesus was so patently obvious.

The Scriptures, regarded as authoritative, rightly understood and taught in the power of the Holy Spirit in this 'apostolic' manner (i.e., interpreted in the light of Jesus as the Messiah) will always form the basis of a united church.

The next outstanding feature of the Jerusalem church was the *fellowship* that existed between its members. This word (*koinonia* in Greek) has become so debased in Christian jargon that it has come to mean no more than a cup of tea, a biscuit and a chat with Mrs Jones after the service. In Acts chapter 2, verse 42, it has the definite article preceding it – '*the* fellowship'. Some newer churches have adopted the word 'fellowship' as part of their name, for example my own church, 'The Fellowship of the King'. For many Christians, the word has become synonymous with 'church'. But here in Acts, it has a more general meaning. It actually means *sharing*. In his commentary on Acts, I. H. Marshall sees it as referring to a common meal (cf v.46) or to a shared religious experience.[4] It could refer to the sharing of goods practised in the church (vv.44–5). Most likely, it refers to the *totality of the believers' shared life together*. They actually were *physically* together. They often met together, shared each other's homes, and showed hospitality to one another. Some House Churches nowadays have emphasised the importance of church members living near one another or even sharing houses. This 'carpet slipper' principle means that Christians should be able to 'pop in on' one another by just walking up the street and into a nearby house, giving encouragement and support where this is needed.

The believers were also together *spiritually*. They had a shared experience of God and of the reality of his supernatural power breaking into their lives. As we have seen, Luke describes them as being 'one in heart and mind' (Acts 4.32). It is this unity at the deepest level of our being that God desires for his people.

We are told that *they had everything in common* (v.44). This does not refer to an enforced 'communism'. It points to the voluntary pooling and sharing of resources and possessions. This arose spontaneously in the hearts of the Christians. It was a practical overflow of the love of God filling them. An integral part of this was their giving to the needy in the church (v.45). There was a movement of money and goods around the church to the people who needed them most.

In our society, where life is geared to privacy – 'the

Englishman's house is his castle' – in many areas, there is a 'drawbridge mentality'; it is not normal to let a neighbour through the front door, much less lend him our garden tools. This fundamentally worldly mentality has penetrated deeply into the church. We are often as loath to share our possessions as any of our non-Christian neighbours. In fact, some of them have a lesson to teach us in this respect. But in a church where the Holy Spirit is creating true fellowship, hearts, homes and pockets will start to open so that those in need will be helped.

We read that *'they broke bread in their homes and ate together with glad and sincere hearts'* (v.46). This implies two things: that they showed hospitality to each other, and that they celebrated a simple and informal type of Holy Communion in one another's homes. The home played a vital part in the development of first-century Christianity.[5] Aquila and Priscilla were probably the most notable Christians who set up 'home groups' (as we would call them), for example in Rome (Romans 16.3). Nympha is also mentioned as having a church in her house (Col. 4.15). There are various examples of new converts showing hospitality to Paul, e.g. Lydia (Acts 16.15) and Titius Justus (Acts 18.7).

The Jerusalem church probably did not often need to show hospitality to travelling apostles, but they did operate an open-house policy when it came to entertaining. Shared meals were the order of the day. In a church where true fellowship is being established, there will, I believe, always be this sort of hospitality freely shown.

Holy Communion appears in the Jerusalem church to have been associated with these shared meals. It was probably a simple, informal act of worship recalling the death, the Resurrection and the presence of the Lord. By the time the church was established in Corinth, it had become part of a meal for a much larger gathering, which, by implication, was not held in a home but in a hall (I Cor. 11.18–22).

It is almost self-evident that Holy Communion will be

49

present at the very centre of any unified fellowship of Christians. Who leads it, and precisely how it happens, is probably a good deal less important than we would like to think. The essential thing is that it does happen. It is tragic that such a potent symbol of our unity as Christians should have become a point – perhaps the most crucial point – of deep denominational division between us.

We also read that *'they devoted themselves . . . to prayer'* (Cor. 2.42). That it was a strong, united and purposeful prayer is shown by the account in I Corinthians chapter 4, verses 23 to 31, of the prayer that followed the release of Peter and John from the Sanhedrin. The burden of the prayer was that the apostles should preach boldly and perform healings and miracles in the name of Jesus (vv.29–30). Such was the power of the prayer, and the dynamism of God's response, that the meeting place was shaken and the believers were once again filled with the Holy Spirit (v.31).

A truly united church will be a praying church. Prayer is the Christian's means of communication with God. It involves talking to God and listening to him. Any Christian can join with another Christian in doing this, across barriers of rank, class, race or denomination. Many Christians have experienced their prejudices melt away as they have prayed with others of different traditions and have discovered the Spirit linking their hearts supernaturally.

We know too that the Jerusalem Christians loved to *worship*, 'praising God' (v.47). We do not know any details of the worship of the Jerusalem church. We know simply that they were a praising community. In praise and worship we focus our attention away from ourselves and onto God. We contemplate Jesus, and in doing so are captivated by him and changed inwardly (as Paul promises us) into his likeness by his Holy Spirit 'with ever-increasing glory' (II Cor. 3.18). True worship is thus profoundly necessary for us as individuals and as churches.

Any church or group of churches seeking unity will

have to come to a point of unity in worship. Christians who acknowledge the reality and presence of the Lord will want to praise and worship him irrespective of how they are feeling at the time. They will be so caught up in him that they will be 'lost in wonder, love and praise'. There will be no room for those who hold back. Many of us will have to lose our prejudices about such matters as clapping or raising hands. On the other hand, it may sometimes be necessary for those of us who are more demonstrative to hold back out of love for the 'weaker brother' (I Cor. 8.9). In general, though, we all need to heed Paul's words to the Romans: 'Offer your bodies as living sacrifices, holy and pleasing to God – this is your spiritual act of worship' (Romans 12.1). True worship is to offer ourselves totally to God. If each of us does that, we shall be united with God and with one another.

The Jerusalem church was also united in expecting *miracles* to happen – and they did (v.43). The apostles' preaching included the miraculous as an integral part of the gospel: 'Jesus of Nazareth was a man accredited by God to you by miracles, wonders and signs, which God did among you through him, as you yourselves know' (Acts 2.22). But the apostles didn't simply live on their past experiences of Jesus' healing ministry. They themselves went out to preach, heal and cast out demons. In doing this they were fulfilling Jesus' command (Matt. 10.8). The healing of the crippled beggar (Acts 3.1–9) was the sort of thing of which Peter and John already had plenty of experience. This time, Jesus was no longer present on earth to report back to. They were relying instead on the power and authority of the Holy Spirit to heal in the name of Jesus.

We are recovering the dimension of divine healing, deliverance and the miraculous in our Western church. Our so-called 'scientific world-view' has blinded us to the possibility of the Holy Spirit filling us and using us as channels of healing to others. The ministry of the American teacher and healer John Wimber has been an enormous help in this respect. He has not simply taught about the Spirit's power, but has publicly demonstrated that power in action. I remember vividly at the 'Acts 86' conference in Birmingham (July 1986)[6] hearing a Swiss doctor testify incredulously about the miraculous lengthening of her leg. This was no superstitious, gullible person but a scientifically trained, intelligent professional who was aware how much shorter one leg had been than the other – and how God had lengthened it by exactly the right amount. Wimber also has the great gift of being down-to-earth and humourous in his approach. He effectively demystifies what is going on when the Holy Spirit moves upon a large gathering by explaining what is happening (which may include considerable numbers of people shaking, falling over, weeping or laughing). He assures his audience that these manifestations are all typical responses to the Spirit's presence, signs of release and blessing. Finally, he interviews members of the congregation who have been healed, encouraging them to say how they feel, and what has happened to them. He always uses low-key, non-religious language in his explanations.

A truly united church will be open to supernatural manifestations of God's power. However controversial this statement may be, I believe it to be true because it is scriptural. But, like all other statements in this chapter, it represents an ideal towards which Christians in the UK are working. We are, by and large, sceptical, lacking in faith. This attitude is sinful and fruitless. We need to have a higher awareness of God's supernatural power. There are welcome signs that this is happening. Local churches are increasingly sensing a 'new wave' of the Holy Spirit. Some are actually sending teams to other churches to encourage them in this area.

Deliverance ministry (the casting-out of evil spirits) is even more controversial than healing, because of its lurid and somewhat medieval overtones. Thanks to my liberal, middle-of-the-road Anglican background, I had not heard much preached about the devil. By the end of my theological training, I was certain that he was merely a mythological personification of all that is evil. It wasn't until a few years later, when I had suddenly become much more aware of the reality of the Holy Spirit, that I began to sense much more strongly the power and presence of an evil intelligence that I had no qualms about calling Satan, the Accuser.

I have already mentioned my experience of deliverance ministry soon after I was 'baptised in the Holy Spirit' in Cambridge. It was during this period that I became convinced of the existence of a spiritual realm of evil, and of the battle that Christians are called to wage against it. By far the most exciting part of the process was that at the name of Jesus the demons had to go! This has been my experience every time since then that I have had to pray in this way. The situation on the particular occasion I have described was not helped by the fact that the Dean of the young man's college had just been one of the signatories of a letter sent by a number of distinguished Cambridge academics to *The Times* stating that the devil and demons were part of the medieval baggage of Christianity that needed to be discarded. Normally, I would have referred this type of situation straight back to my colleague in the other college, but, given his views, I felt unable to on this occasion.

The miraculous power of God also has a negative aspect: supernatural judgment. This is not a popular subject with Christians, understandably. The account of the deaths of Ananias and Sapphira in Acts chapter 5, verse 1 to 11, has upset many. Would the God who is love really act like that? The answer is that in a situation where there is such a high degree of openness, reality, love and trust in the community of God's people, lying to the Holy Spirit brings its own judgment. It is never actually stated that God struck Ananias and Sapphira down. It is more likely that they were so devastated by Peter's open statement of their guilt (by supernatural knowledge) and their inner conviction of sin, that they died. Their sin was to break fellowship radically with God and their fellow-believers. In a church where there was such a high quality of unity, this brought shattering results. As a result, 'great fear seized the whole church' (v.11). The fear was a holy awe at the presence of God so powerfully manifested in judgment.

I know of a similar, though less drastic contemporary example of this in a London church where the Spirit is powerfully at work. A girl became rigid during a service, and quite unable to move. When the church leaders came over to pray for her, it became clear that she was full of unforgiveness for someone. She refused to forgive the person, and eventually had to be carried from the church. Later, however, she repented, and forgave; immediately, she was able to move normally again.

Fellowship within a truly united church will not be broken without severe consequences for the sinner. It may be necessary to impose discipline lovingly, but the main discipline will come from the powerful presence of the Holy Spirit in the community.

Finally, we may ask what was the response of the people of Jerusalem to the existence of such a dynamic church in their midst? Many viewed it with favour. The Jerusalem church was very successful by the standards of church growth in Britain today. It grew to twenty-five its original size after the first evangelistic sermon had been preached and continued to increase at a tremendous rate: 'The number of men' (i.e. not including women or children) 'grew to about five thousand' (Acts 4.4). Everything about the Jerusalem church was consistent with their faith. Their love, their united fellowship, their lifestyle, the power of the Holy Spirit working through them, their prayer and worship, their generosity and compassion all underlined the truth of what they preached. They did not need a big evangelistic campaign. They just were themselves. As a result, many joined them. They did not have to try hard: 'The Lord added to their number daily those who were being saved' (Acts 2.47). Even those who did not join them still approved of them: 'They enjoyed the favour of all the people.'

A church united in this way will be greatly appreciated by many in the community who may at the same time be frightened of getting too involved because they sense the very real cost of commitment. It is significant that Luke records, 'No one else dared join them, even though they were highly regarded by the people' (Acts 5.13). Exactly the same reaction arises today from a public that is fed up with the unclear lead often given by church spokesmen on the media. The British public respects Christian commitment and the reality of the power of God, even though the majority do not want to be directly challenged by it.

However, at the same time as exciting respect, a totally united and empowered church will arouse *hostility and persecution*. This certainly happened in Jerusalem, where the last thing the powers-that-be wanted was a resurgence of the cult of Jesus of Nazareth after he had effectively been done away with. The apostles were first hauled before the Sanhedrin, the Jewish ruling body, and threatened (Acts 4.11–21). They were then imprisoned but miraculously released (Acts 5.17–20). Next they were flogged and ordered not to preach (Acts 6.40). There followed the stoning of Stephen (Acts 7.54–60) and the great persecution of the Jerusalem church by Saul (Acts 8.1–3).

A lively, thriving church in an alien culture will always be persecuted. The small but growing church in Nepal is a good example. The officially Hindu state does not allow open evangelism, and those who are baptised are liable to a year's imprisonment. Yet the Nepali church continues to grow. It shows many of the characteristics of the Jerusalem church, including evangelistic zeal, healing miracles, and considerable courage.

In a country with a Christian heritage, such as the United Kingdom, the main enemy of the church is apathy. People are generally bored with institutional religion, and like to regard Christians as irrelevant and even hypocritical. But vigorous, evangelistic Christianity instantly stirs up a negative response – often, unfortunately, from within the institutional church. Such persecution is usually subtle and psychological. We have not reached the point where open-air preachers have rotten eggs and even more unpleasant objects thrown at them, as was the case in the early Methodist revival. But as the church becomes more what it ought to be, opposition and persecution are bound to grow in response. 'Everyone who wants to live a godly life in Christ Jesus will be persecuted' (II Tim. 3.12). That was clearly true in the first-century Eastern Mediterranean world where the church was born, suffering the hostility of the Jewish establishment in Jerusalem and of the power of Rome. It could be true in our own nation and day, when apathy has given way to aggression. It would happen if the church became all that it should be, vigorous and united, and if the government were to become actively anti-Christian.

The Jerusalem church gives us the broad outlines of what a truly united church should be like. It does not, however, tell us much in detail about the way members of such a church relate and function together. To understand more about this, we need to turn to the writings of St Paul.

Chapter 5

The Body of Christ

Many different pictures are used by the New Testament writers to describe the church – the temple, God's building, a royal priesthood, the bride of Christ. One picture is used by Paul particularly when he is concerned to show the unity of God's people: that of the *body of Christ*. In this chapter, I want to look at some of the passages where he writes about the church as the body of Christ, find out what he means, and apply this to the local church situation in England at the present time.

First, I Corinthians chapter 12, verses 12 to 31. The point Paul is making here is very simple. He states it in verse 12: 'The body is a unit, though it is make up of many parts; and though all its parts are many, they form one body. So it is with Christ.' The church is Christ's body on earth, and it is made up of many parts. In another letter, Colossians, Paul writes that Christ is the head of the body (Col. 1.18). In I Corinthians chapter 12, he concentrates on the body itself, and he immediately focuses on its unity: 'For we were all baptised by one spirit into one body – whether Jews or Greeks, slave or free – and we were all given the one Spirit to drink' (v. 13).

In this passage, Paul is making some basic points about the unity of the church. He is talking to a local church, i.e, the church in Corinth, but what he says can be applied to any local church:

The first point he makes is that *church unity transcends all known social barriers*. The church at that time was made up of some highly contrasting groups of people. There were Jews, brought up to observe the law of Moses to the letter, with a horror of idol-worship: and Gentiles, familiar with the worship of Greek and Roman gods, not to mention such practices as temple-prostitution, which was rife at Corinth. There were slaves, who had absolutely no rights, rubbing shoulders in the church services with their masters. No other social institution apart from the church could have brought such totally different groupings together. Paul is saying that it was the power of God alone that had done it. Those groups had nothing in common apart from the love of God shown to them through the death and the Resurrection of Jesus Christ. Their unity came from their repentance, faith and baptism. Each of them had individually responded to God's call; they had been baptised and filled with the Holy Spirit. Here in verse 13, baptism is seen not so much as into the *death* of Christ (c.p. Romans 6.4) as into the *body* of Christ, the church. God has entitled each Christian to be a member of his church, and has also given each Christian the same Holy Spirit to drink.

We know that the first generation of Christians didn't find this at all easy to work out in practice. Acts chapters 6, verses 1 to 6, tells us that the Greek-speaking Jews in Jerusalem had a problem with the Hebrew-speaking Jews because their widows were being overlooked in the daily distribution of food. Galatians records Paul's single-minded stand against the pressure put on the Gentile converts in Galatia by Jewish Christians from Jerusalem to conform to Jewish practices, in particular circumcision. That situation led him to oppose Peter publicly, 'because he was clearly in the wrong' (Gal. 2.11). Peter was wrong because he had allowed himself to be pressurised by Jewish Christians not even to eat with Gentile Christians. Paul saw that the essential unity of the church is deeply compromised by this sort of behaviour. Later in the Galatian letter he nails his colours to the mast with one of the most triumphant statements of church unity in the Bible: 'There is neither Jew nor Greek, slave nor free, male nor female, for you are all one in Christ Jesus' (Gal. 3.28). The letter to Philemon makes it clear that all was not plain sailing when it came to reconciling a runaway slave, who had become a Christian after running away, with his Christian master. Paul summons up all his eloquence to appeal to Philemon to accept back the slave, Onesimus, 'no longer as a slave, but better than a slave, as a dear brother' (Philemon 16).

There are probably at least as many divisions in British society today, and these make it as difficult for us to include everyone in the church as it was for the first-century Christians in Corinth. Many churches find it hard to assimilate young people because so many of their members are old (unusually, we have the opposite problem in our church: older folk visiting us tend to be alarmed by the vast numbers of young people, and feel that they wouldn't fit in, although we try to make them as welcome as possible). Some churches have a unhappy knack of making visitors feel outsiders. Often they can't help it, because their very composition excludes large groups of people. All-white churches tend to exclude black people, and vice-versa. Middle-class churches can't easily cope with unemployed punks. The same problem occurs the world over. I recently heard the Soviet Christian rock musician and leader, Valeri Barinov, say that special new Christian 'fellowships' have had to be created to accommodate the large number of young hippies and punks who have recently been converted in Russia. They just don't fit into the conventional church structures.

The ideal local church ought to be able to include all and sundry. Few churches in Britain do, but the Gospel demands that we aim for the best. We need to remember this in urban Britain, with our many 'specialist' churches. We need to realise, as different fellowships in our locality, that we need each other – otherwise, we shall not fulfil the enormous potential that God has put in us.

Paul goes on to show that in fact *church unity encourages diversity*. In I Corinthians chapter 12, verses 15 to 21, he has fun imagining dialogues between various parts of the body. He's making the point that the body has many parts, and that all of them are interdependent. With the benefit of modern science, we know even better than Paul how true this is. Having studied the intricate workings of living cells, scientists know just how delicate the inter-relationships of the minutest parts of the body are, and the Christian marvels at how wonderfully God has put it all together. We can echo David's words in Psalm 139: 'For you created my inmost being; you knit me together in my mother's womb. I praise you because I am fearfully and wonderfully made' (v.14). Inter-relationships within the church are equally intricate yet finely balanced.

In verses to 27 to 28, Paul lists some of the constituent parts of the church (the word 'member' is useful here, as it can be used both of a part of the body and a part of a social unit). These are apostles, prophets, teachers, workers of miracles, healers, helpers, administrators, and those who speak in tongues. On the face of it, this list is a glorious mixture of functions, some more apparently 'supernatural' than others. But we would not make a distinction between 'natural' and 'supernatural' parts of Christ's body. All are supernatural, if God put them there, and if God is inspiring them. There is, for example, a profound difference between a non-Christian and a Christian administrator. The former has to trust solely in his training and expertise. The latter need not have such qualifications, but he can and should expect the insights and inspiration of God if he is actively seeking him. The first treasurer of our church was not an accountant, but he had the sure touch of one who had been gifted by God for that particular task.

Paul, then, is clear that diversity in the church is to be welcomed. Unity is not a bland uniformity, with every Christian conforming to a stereotype, but a rich composite of the varied personalities, gifts and ministries of each member.

Lastly, *church unity means that every Christian matters because we need each other.* Paul is concerned to point out the interdependence of each member of the body of Christ. He admits that some parts of the body seem to be weaker and even 'less honourable' (I Cor. 12.23), but states that, through combining the members, God wants to strengthen the weaker ones, 'so that there should be no division in the body, but that its parts should have equal concern for each other' (v.25). Each part of the body is, in fact, indispensable. He makes the identical point in Romans chapter 12, verses 3 to 8, where again he is talking about the body of Christ and the function of members and their gifts within it. As in I Corinthians chapter 12, he stresses the diversity of gifts and the interdependence of members: 'Just as each of us has one body with many members, and these members do not all have the same function, so in Christ we who are many form one body, and each member belongs to all the others' (v.4–5). The list of gifts that follows are mostly not obviously 'supernatural', with the exception of prophecy. But again, we are wrong to make the distinction; serving, teaching, encouraging, giving, leading, and showing mercy are all supernatural if God is inspiring the people who are gifted in that way.

This perspective on the church and church unity is very different from what many of us are used to. Instead of a typical situation where the vicar or minister does everything, and is expected to manifest all of the gifts within the Church, Paul expects his church to be a living organism in which every member is contributing his or her invaluable gift. Jealousy is ruled out, because we should be so appreciative of one another that we are continually thanking and encouraging one another. I know from experience how vulnerable a leader feels when he or she starts to delegate, and to encourage members of the church to exercise their ministry, but the results show that the pain is well worth it in the end. It is, in fact, a great relief and a joy to encourage others to come into their ministry, and to relax in the knowledge that you don't have to do everything after all, but can concentrate on your essential ministry of leadership – which may, when all's said and done, consist mainly of prayer, preaching, envisioning, and leading by example.

Actually, what Paul is teaching is even more radical than this! If we look back at I Corinthians chapter 12, this time at verses 7 to 11, we see that there are certain 'manifestations' of the spirit (i.e., instant or transient gifts of the Spirit – verse 7) which, he implies, any Christian can have 'for the common good' whenever God wills. These are the ninefold gifts of wisdom, knowledge, faith, healing, miracles, prophecy, discernment, tongues and interpretation (I don't think that this list is necessarily meant to be exhaustive, though it seems quite long as it is!). So, for example, anyone can receive and transmit a gift of healing when they pray for a fellow Christian who is ill – they don't have to be someone with a regular healing ministry in the church.

This gives an insight into how a ministry develops. If a person consistently shows a particular manifestation from God over a period of time (e.g., praying for the sick and regularly seeing healings), it becomes clear that they are developing a gift of healing. But it also points to the gloriously free and generous way in which God bestows his gifts. No Christian is more qualified than another to receive a gift. The most important thing is that we are able to ask for it, receive it, and then step out in faith and use it. Paul concludes, 'All these (manifestations) are the work of one and the same spirit, and he gives them to each one, just as he determines' (v.11). Finally, let's notice again that every manifestation of the spirit is given 'for the common good', i.e. to bring blessing to the church, which includes strengthening its unity.

The other significant passage in the New Testament which deals with the unity of the body is Ephesians chapter 4, verses 1 to 16. Here, Paul looks first at *unity in calling and character* (v.1–6). In verses 4 to 6, Paul makes some great statements about Christian unity. There is, he writes, 'one body and one spirit – just as you were called to one hope when you were called – one Lord, one faith, one baptism; one God and Father of all, who is over all and through all and in all.' Our calling is to one hope, the hope of heaven; being with God for ever, doing his will perfectly, enjoying his love fully. This involves all the other unities of which Paul writes. Notice the exclusiveness of these claims. If there is only one body, it is wrong to think of denominations as being God's best or ultimate aim. If there is only one Spirit, Christians cannot have anything to do with religious experiences that do not involve the Holy Spirit. If there is only one Lord, Christians cannot give loyalty to any other god or idol, whether religious or human. If there is only one faith, biblical faith in Jesus as Lord, Christians cannot flirt with any philosophy which denies it. If there is only one baptism, we need to come to a common mind about what we understand baptism to mean and to involve.

However, Paul doesn't encourage the Ephesians to rejoice in their unity, sit back, and do nothing about it. He begs them earnestly, 'Make every effort to keep the unity of the Spirit in the bond of peace' (v.3). Some Christians seem to have an unreal and indeed unbiblical attitude to unity. I have often heard people say, in soulful and super-spiritual tones, 'Isn't it wonderful that when the Lord looks down on Bristol he sees one church!' I'm not sure that I can be so certain what the Lord sees when he looks down on Bristol (or anywhere else). But I believe that God is a realist. He does not, cannot, rejoice in a unity that does not actually exist. He is well aware of the sin of disunity in his Church, and he cannot bear it. This is why Christians have to exhort one another, as Paul does here, to make every effort to keep that unity which is God's wonderful gift to us. Jesus won it for us on the cross (Eph. 2.15). It is our responsibility to enter into the reality of it. Church history has proved that if we don't, we very easily lose it.[1]

What Paul has already said in verses 1 and 2 actually logically follows on from this. Because of the unity that we have by faith, we need to make an effort to hold on to it. That means in practice living in a certain way, 'worthy of the calling you have received' (v.1). In verse 2 he gives an example of what he means: 'be completely humble and gentle; be patient, bearing with one another in love.' Here we reach the heart of what unity in the body of Christ is all about. We shall only be truly one when we have Christ's character fully formed within us. To put it another way: we need to show in our lives the *fruit* of the Holy Spirit. Doing this will actually require effort

63

– persevering prayer, and self-disciplined behaviour. If each of us is bearing this fruit of the Lord's character in our lives, the unity of the Spirit is bound to be established among us as we love one another with his love.

The fruits of the spirit mentioned here include, first, *humility.* Jesus taught his disciples a clear lesson about servanthood, not just from what he said but even more from his example. He washed their feet so that they might wash one another's feet (John 13.14). But this wasn't an outward, dramatic gesture with no reference to reality. Jesus' servanthood sprang from a heart-attitude of humility. He did not even consider his position within the Godhead as something to be clung on to (Phil. 2.6). Paul teaches so well from Jesus' example: 'Do nothing out of selfish ambition or vain conceit, but in humility consider others better than yourselves' (Phil. 2.3). 'Better' means 'more important', i.e. we should put others' interests before our own. Have you ever tried to do that? It doesn't come easily. In the church, there is so much ambition: wanting to be 'up front', to be noticed and listened to. Those of us who are engaged in high-profile ministries where we sit on platforms and are much in the public eye need to be particularly ruthless with ourselves about our real motives. Whose glory are we seeking, God's or our own? Conversely, if we do not have a particularly spectacular ministry, we need to beware of ambitiously seeking any position in the church or society which would bolster our ego rather than serving our fellow-Christians.

Gentleness is a word which is also translated 'meekness'. Jesus' attitude to the needy and defenceless was characterised by this quality, e.g. in his encounter with the woman taken in adultery (John 8.1–11), with the woman with the haemorrhage (Mark 5.25–34), and with children (Mark 10.13–6). We are reminded never to take a high-and-mighty attitude with people who are less gifted or needier than we are. All of us feel tempted to talk to the more attractive, interesting and lively members of the church rather than the people we find dull and off-putting. The trouble is that this attitude leads to cliques which ignore some people altogether. We need to resist it firmly.

Patience is the ability to forbear, to be long-suffering – to put up with awkward people and situations without getting upset and angry. It is closely linked to the divine quality of forgiveness. Paul was very conscious of this aspect of God's love. He wrote, 'I was shown mercy so that in me, the worst of sinners, Christ Jesus might display his unlimited patience as an example for those who would believe in him and receive eternal life' (I Tim. 1.16). God can work that patience into our character if we let him. I find that I very often have to put up with some very difficult people, situations and remarks in the church. Indeed, I sometimes think I could fill a notebook with the discouraging things that have been said to me after services (though I am glad to say that I could fill a much bigger notebook with the encouraging things, thanks to the many lovely and sensitive Christians in our church). I'm afraid that when people say negative things to me, I have a tendency to take them personally and to 'bite back'. Probably quite a number of Christians have to struggle with this. It is very human and understandable, but it is clearly wrong! Those of us who have a problem with this particular sin need to confess it to God, ask for his forgiveness and cleansing, and forgive the person who has hurt us (the process I described in more detail in the last chapter). We need to ask God to use such situations to make us more long-suffering. I have found over the years that God has helped me become more able to cope in a loving and patient way with confrontations when they arise.

Next comes *love*. This work, the Greek *agape*, refers to the self-sacrificing love of God that is prepared to die for enemies as well as for friends. It is the greatest and most enduring fruit of the Spirit (I Cor. 13.13). In a very similar passage in Colossians 3, after giving a list of spiritual fruit, and encouraging his readers to forgive one another, Paul writes, 'Over all these virtues put on love, which binds them all together in perfect unity' (v. 14). In other words, love is the quality which unites all the other fruit of the Spirit, rather as the ground bass of a great musical work undergirds the rest of the orchestra. The church needs to be a society where the love of God is clearly present: not just human affection, though that should certainly develop, but that supernatural love which can cause people of very different temperaments and backgrounds to be deeply committed to one another. In our own church, I can think of people that I used to find very difficult whom I now love dearly and count as my friends. We have been through a lot together, and have, in the process, hurt each other. But because we have the love of Christ in our hearts, we have forgiven one another and moved into a new depth of relationship. Peter, who had sinned much and been forgiven much, knew this well. He writes, 'Above all, love one another, because love covers over a multitude of sins' (I Peter 4.8) – including the sin of disunity and division in the local church, once there is repentance.

We need to remember, too, that love is not an 'optional extra' for Christians. When Jesus said to his disciples, 'Love one another as I have loved you', he described this as a 'new commandment' (John 13.34). Love of this sort – the Jesus sort – was to be the hallmark of all his followers. We need to ask ourselves regularly whether we are keeping this commandment of the Lord's, or flagrantly disobeying it.

Finally, *peace*: 'Make every effort to keep the unity of the spirit in the bond of peace' (Eph. 4.3). For Paul, Christians are actually bonded together by the peace of God as well as by his love. Why is this? We can find the clue in another statement of Paul's: 'Do not be anxious about anything, but in everything, by prayer and petition, with thanksgiving, present your request to God. And the peace of God, which transcends all understanding, will guard your hearts and your minds in Christ Jesus' (Phil. 4.6–7). If we allow ourselves to be anxious, we are admitting that we don't trust God. This is human and understandable, but sinful. A church full of anxious people is a church that has cut itself off from the source of peace, namely God. As a result, relationships within the church will become fragmented and fraught. A break in our 'vertical' unity with God tends to result in a breakdown of our 'horizontal' unity with one another. If we discipline ourselves to repent of this untrusting attitude, we will sense God's care, his security and his peace once more. We will regain peace with our fellow-Christians, and be bonded together in unity.

From this passage, then, we see that the various fruits of the Spirit are bonds that join the different members of the body together – the 'supporting ligaments', as Paul puts in verse 16. To do this, they have to be used. Fruit has to be tasted to be enjoyed, otherwise it will rot. Ligaments have to exercised, or they will atrophy and cease to be of any use. A church whose members are actively being humble, gentle, long-suffering, loving and peaceful will be a united church.

Paul now goes on to look at *unity in ministry and maturity* (Eph 4.7–16). He has shown that Christ has established unity in the Church, and that we have to make an effort to make it real. But there is a more perfect unity in store for the Church. In verses 7 to 16, Paul is looking forward to the mature unity between Christians which is coming in the future. *Growing into Union* was the name of a book about Anglican-Methodist unity.[2] The title accurately describes a process which should, in fact, be happening within every local church, as well as between churches or denominations. Paul's message is that, as far as unity is concerned, the best is yet to be – provided that certain elements are present in the Church.

The first of these is a *basic range of ministries*. Jesus ascended into heaven to, among other things, give gifts to his church through pouring his Spirit upon us. Among his most important gifts are the four ministries mentioned here (v.11) – apostles, prophets, evangelists, and pastors and teachers.

There has been a great debate recently over whether the first two ministries in this list are still in operation in the church. In Ephesians chapter 2, verse 20, Paul writes that the church is 'built upon the foundation of the apostles and prophets'. Some would see this as implying

67

that apostles and prophets only functioned in the first generation of the Church, in order to lay the original foundations of a building that has been growing ever since. While agreeing that there was something unique about the ministry of the Twelve as well as of Paul and the other apostles mentioned in the New Testament, I would personally want to maintain that there is still a clear apostolic and prophetic ministry in the church today. Apostles seem essentially to have a foundation-laying, church-planting role in the church. Wherever the gospel breaks new ground, there is need of those with an apostolic ministry to plough up the hard earth and establish new churches. We might prefer to call much people 'pioneer missionaries' or 'church-planters', but whatever we call them, they clearly have an apostolic function. Moreover, apostles do not operate just in countries where the gospel has never been preached before. Because every generation, even in a so-called 'Christian country' like Britain, must be re-envangelised, we need apostles in those countries too. In Britain, for example, leaders engaged in planting new churches on vast housing estates clearly have an apostolic role in what is in fact a post-Christian, secular culture.

As far as the other three ministries are concerned, we are familiar with evangelists and pastors/teachers. What about prophets? According to the Bible, a prophet is someone who has 'stood in the council of the Lord' (Jer. 23.18), i.e., who is so close to the heart of God that God can use him to transmit God's word to the Church and to the world. Christian prophets seem in the New Testament to speak largely to the church. For example, Agabus predicts 'through the Spirit' that there will be a severe famine in the Roman Empire (Acts 11:28). A prophet nowadays could well speak God's word to the church in this sort of way. To be able to do this, he (or she) would have to be a person of prayer, someone who is prepared to spend time with God so as to hear accurately what God wants said. A prophet also has to be humble, for Scripture tells us that prophecy needs to be tested carefully (I Thess. 5.20–1), and he has to be prepared to submit himself to that. If the church does not accept what he says, he has to put up with it! This is the church's responsibility, and they will have to take the consequences, ultimately answering to God for their decision.

I believe that prophets clearly do exist in the church in this country at the present time. They exercise an invaluable ministry in speaking God's word to the church. The importance of prophecy is indicated by the fact that it is the only gift or ministry to be included in all the main lists of gifts in the New Testament. If a leader senses a prophetic gift developing in a church member and believes it to be genuine, he should nurture that gift, not sit on it. We need to remember that immediately before urging the Thessalonians to test prophecy, Paul writes, 'Do not put out the Spirit's fire; do not treat prophecies with comtempt' (I Thess. 5.19–20). Have we ever done either of those things?

We shall return to these ministries in more detail in the final chapter, when looking more closely at the future dimension of Christian unity. There is, however, a second element that has to be present in the church if perfect unity is to be achieved. Paul writes that Christ gives the ministries to the church 'to prepare God's people for *works of service*' (Eph. 4.12). He makes the important point that Christians will never grow into maturity if they don't do the works of righteousness that God requires of them. Jesus actually wants us to show our love and concern for other Christians in all sorts of practical ways, like sharing our money, our possessions and our homes. I am writing this at a time when we have had a lot of guests staying in our home. It has been a strain for us to entertain, because of all sorts of pressures (not least writing a book!), but it has been worth it. God has given us the opportunity of opening our home to our friends in this way, and in so doing we have received a blessing.

If we are going to go out into the world proclaiming the gospel of Jesus Christ, being prepared to heal the sick, cast out demons, and share our love and concern in ways which are demanding and draining on our time and energies, we need first to know what it is to do 'works of service' for one another in the church. Some Christians seem to expect the world to revolve round them. They are quick to criticise faults in others, but seem unwilling to get involved in the nitty-gritty of serving their fellow-Christians. Actually, we all have that tendency. We need to take to heart Paul's words to the Galatians: 'As we have opportunity, let us do good to all people, especially to those who belong to the family of believers'(Gal. 5.10).

The final element that needs to be present in the church for future unity to be achieved is *truthful speech.* 'Speaking the truth in love, we will in all things grow up into him who is the Head, that is, Christ'(Eph. 4.15). In my experience, truthful speech is an absolute necessity if Christians are to achieve a unity that is mature and lasting. If we have a difficulty or disagreement with someone, the temptation is either to suppress it or to talk about it with someone other than the person concerned. Either way, we are doing the wrong thing. Suppression will cause the problem to erupt later in a much stronger form. Talking to someone else may be helpful in the short term, but usually only if it leads to eventual confrontation – otherwise, we will simply be talking behind someone else's back. Almost invariably, it is confrontation that is needed. We need to be truthful and open with one another at all times: 'Each of you must put off falsehood and speak truthfully to his neighbour, for we are all member of one body' (Eph. 4.25). However, we must prepare for confrontation carefully, to make sure that we do it in love. We should examine ourselves to make sure that our motives are right, that we have confessed to God any wrong attitudes we may have towards the other person, and that we have forgiven them for the wrong that has hurt us.

Such openness can lead to conflict, but conflict is not necessarily a bad thing. In her book *Conflict: Friend or Foe?,* Joyce Huggett makes the helpful point that conflict can be very positive if used in the right way.[3]

We need to remember that Paul links truthful speech with love. Joyce Huggett sees that if there is a conflict between Christians, we should first communicate with one another about it (speaking truthfully). In the process of this communication, we may need to clarify any misunderstanding or mis-communication that may have arisen. All this needs to be done against a background of loving commitment. If the process is handled in the right way, it will result in growth. Joyce Huggett expresses this as an equation: 'conflict + communication + clarification + commitment = growth.'

Team leadership is being seen more and more as a New Testament pattern that we need to rediscover. In our own church, I am trying to build up a strong team of young leaders with complementary gifts. In the process, however, we are discovering one another's weaknesses as well as our strengths! Sometimes there are explosions as a result, and all our resources of love and forgiveness are tapped. Such difficulties, and the way we resolve them, are an inevitable part of a process of growth into a strong, committed, loving and united leadership.

The same will be true of all our relationships within the church. As God brings closer unity, through the operation of spiritual gifts and ministries, and through the growth and outworking of the fruit of the Holy Spirit, Christians will inevitably get to know each other better, warts and all. More openness will bring a welcome breath of reality into our relationships, but also greater friction. Isn't it amazing how we Christians expect each other to be perfect? We impose the highest standards on one another, yet expect to receive deep and sensitive understanding of our own problems.

The fact is that we are redeemed sinners, who are still working out in our daily lives what it is to 'die to sin and live to righteousness' (I Peter 2.24). If we face the conflict that truthfulness brings, confessing our sins to God and to one another, forgiving and receiving forgiveness, asking God for grace to go on loving one another, and determined to press through into new depths of relationship with our fellow Christians, we shall indeed

71

grow into a unity that nothing can shake. Ephesians chapter 4, verse 16, implies that it is not just the people with ministry gifts who are responsible for the growth of the church. Each member of the body has to do his or her work. We are all involved. The theme of I Corinthians chapter 12, is not far away.

We have seen, then, that a number of elements are basic to unity in the local church, and indeed to Christian unity on any scale. There must be a diversity of spiritual gifts and ministries working together for the common good. There must be spiritual fruit in people's lives that is expressed in actual acts of righteousness. There must be loving yet truthful communication in situations of conflict so that disunity may be resolved. Finally, we cannot opt out of our responsibilities, because the body of Christ includes each one of us.

Chapter 6

The Family of God

The bus had deposited me in the centre of the small town of Edinboro, near Erie, Pennsylvania, USA. Jetlagged after an Atlantic crossing and two domestic flights, I found myself standing in front of a large, rather ramshackle-looking house. The door opened, and I was greeted warmly by a young man who turned out to be a student at the local art college. He was living in a community of Christians; the house was one of the key 'community-households'. In it lived twelve or so young men, some in full-time church work, some students, some with jobs in the town.

I spent the night on a surprisingly comfortable bunk-bed in the attic, which acted as a communal dormitory, and was awakened at six a.m. when an alarm-clock sounded and twelve bleary-eyed young men rose to wash, dress and stagger downstairs to have half an hour's communal prayer and worship before some of them had to go to work. Breakfast was a simple meal of cereals and milk made with powder (so much for my ideas of American Christians' affluence!). I questioned the lads about their lifestyle, and found that they pooled all their money and drew from a communal kitty. A few of them had been Christians for a long time, but most were recent converts. There was a household leader, responsible to the leaders of the community for what went on in the house. It turned out that he had been the leading drug-pusher at the art college before he was converted, two years previously. The impact of his conversion had been such that many of his friends had since become Christians too.

The community consisted of several similar households, both male and female (but not mixed), as well as young married couples (some with single people living with them), many of whom lived in mobile homes. Food was bought, and laundry washed, communally (clothes got muddled up – a week later I saw one of my shirts going down the street on someone else's back!). Community members were also members of various local churches, of all denominations (including RC), which they attended on Sundays, but they also attended their main community service, which was on a Wednesday evening.

I was impressed by what I saw. There was a strong sense of love and commitment to Jesus and to one another. Young Christians were being very effectively and gently discipled. Converts were being made through coffee-bar outreach. The community had a good name in the town, particularly because of their work with delinquent teenagers, which was officially approved by the Police Department. I had never seen such radical sharing of money, property and real affection. There was a disarming openness, coupled with a lack of heavy authoritarianism. As I lay in bed in a state of semi-wakefulness before the alarm went off, I seemed to hear God say, audibly, 'I delight in this place'.

We have looked at the picture of the church as the *body of Christ*. But there is another picture which the New Testament uses to show the church in all the attractiveness of true unity: the *family of God*. The community of young Christians that I stayed with in rural Pennsylvania was a shining example of the sort of Christian family which the church ought to be.

There are two words translated 'family' in the New Testament. The first is only once used of the church, in Ephesians chapter 3, verse 15. Paul writes (v.14), 'For this reason I kneel before the Father, from whom his whole *family* in heaven and on earth derives its name.' The word can be translated 'fatherhood', and here it clearly refers to God as Father of his whole church. The Old Testament writers, particularly the prophets, saw Israel, in general, as God's son, though usually as a rebellious one (e.g. Jeremiah 3.4ff.). But Jesus with great originality emphasised that God can personally be addressed as 'Father' by an individual. The New Testament scholar Joachim Jeremias writes,

'To his disciples it must have been something quite extraordinary that Jesus addressed God as "my Father".'[1]

Even more remarkably, Jesus used a particular Aramaic word, 'Abba', to address God in prayer. We know this because the word is actually quoted by Mark in his account of the prayer in Gethsemane (Mark 14.36): '"Abba, Father," he said "everything is possible for you".' 'Abba' was the familiar word used by Jews of Jesus' time, both children and adults, to address their own fathers. It is difficult to translate – 'daddy' is too childish for some of us, while 'dad' sounds to others a bit too familiar. Have you ever tried using 'dad' or 'daddy' in your own prayers? You might find it helpful. At any rate, 'Abba' to a Jew had a warmth and a familiarity about it. But one thing is clear: no Jew would ever have used the word in addressing God. To have done so would have seemed presumptuous and irreverant.

Yet Jesus did use it in speaking to his heavenly Father. To me, this is clear proof that the incarnate Jesus was well aware of his unique relationship with God as the Son, the second person of the Trinity. But Jesus did something even more revolutionary: he invited his disciples to address God as 'Abba' too. We know this from Luke's shorter version of the Lord's Prayer (Luke 11.2–4), in which Jesus teaches the disciples to pray simply 'Father', the Greek equivalent of 'Abba'.

This blends perfectly with Jesus' teaching on discipleship. First he stresses the radical break that a true disciple would have to make with his or her natural family: '"If anyone comes to me and does not hate his father and mother, his wife and children, his brothers and sisters – yes, even his own life – he cannot be my disciple"' (Luke 14.26). Commentators point out that the word 'hate' here should be understood in its Semitic sense of 'to love less than', though it could also mean 'to renounce'.[2] Either way, the point is clear: a true disciple of Jesus will make following him a higher priority than any family ties. As a reward for this, however, the disciple will find that he has become a member of a new family: '"I tell you the truth . . . no one who has left home or brothers or sisters or mother or father or children or fields for me and the Gospel will fail to receive a hundred times as much in this present age (homes, brothers, sisters, mothers, children and fields – and with them, persecutions) and in the age to come, eternal life"' (Mark 10.29–30). This vast family is clearly the family of God, made up of those who can call God 'Abba'.

This was part of Paul's teaching, too. First, he saw that each individual Christian has entered by faith into the same relationship of sonship with God through Christ. No matter that it is adopted sonship; it is no less real for that. Significantly, Paul uses the very same, unique word that Jesus used to express, this time, the Christian's relationship with the Father; '. . . You received the Spirit of sonship. And by him we cry "*Abba*, Father". The Spirit himself testifies with our spirit that we are God's children' (Romans 8.15–6). Second, he saw that this applies to all Christians: 'You are all sons of God through faith in Christ Jesus' (Gal. 3.26). Here, he used the word 'sons' rather than 'sons and daughters' to express the fact that each Christian has the rights and inheritance of a first-born son. But it is clear from the pastoral letters that sees this principle worked out in the church community in terms of family relationships: 'Do not rebuke an older man harshly, but exhort him as if he were your father. Treat younger men as brothers, older women as mothers, and younger women as sisters, with absolute purity' (I Tim. 5: 1–2)

Both Jesus and Paul, then, teach that the church is a huge family, of which God is the supreme Father, and that relationships within it are actually more binding than those within our natural families (apart, that is, from marriage – Paul teaches clearly that even in a marriage between a Christian and a non-Christian, the Christian partner may not leave the non-Christian – I Cor. 7.12–6). The other word for 'family' makes this point even more strongly. It means simply 'house' or 'household', and is much the more common of the two words. In the context of the early church, a 'household' was a lot bigger than a family unit in twentieth century

Britain. Where we would think of a married couple with, on average, two or three children, the New Testament household would have included certainly a couple with children, but with the probable addition of grandparents, other dependent relatives, and slaves. Cornelius' 'household' (Acts 11.14) consisted of relatives and close friends, a group described as a 'large gathering' (Acts 10.27). Some of them he had called together (10.24); others, presumably, lived in his house. So when Paul writes of the Church as 'God's household' (e.g., Eph. 2.19; Gal. 6.10), he is thinking very much of what we would call an 'extended family'.

At the same time, Jesus and Paul both emphasise the uniqueness and indissolubility of the marriage bond. Jesus, when questioned about marriage, repeats the words from Genesis which speak of man and woman becoming 'one flesh' (2.24), and gives the solemn command, 'What God has joined together let man not separate' (Matt. 19.6). Paul compares marriage to the relationship between Christ and the Church (Eph. 5.22–3), and he, too, quotes the Genesis passage. Also, Paul teaches clearly that Christian parents have a particular responsibility for bringing up their children, and that children should respect their parents (e.g., Eph. 6.1–4). How then does this teaching fit into the wider picture of the Church as God's true family?

The two emphases can't be contradictory. If we look first at the idea of the church as God's family, we see a wonderful picture of a committed, close-knit group who love and support each other in every way: spiritually, emotionally and practically. As we have already seen, the Jerusalem church portrayed in the early chapters of Acts is a clear example of this sort of family; for me personally, the community in Edinboro was another.

The quality of their relationships is summed up in the word *fellowship* (in Greek, *koinonia*). As we have seen, the root of the word means *communal*: 'it denotes the unanimity and unity brought about by the Spirit. The individual was completely upheld by the community.'[3] These relationships were not upheld by rules and regulations, but by God's love in the heart of each church member. So when, for example, Paul organised a collection of money for the Jerusalem church when it had been hit by famine, he didn't compel the other churches to give. He appealed to their hearts. 'Each man should give what he has decided in his heart to give, not reluctantly or under compulsion, for God loves a cheerful giver' (II Cor. 9.7). Churches that make tithing compulsory should take note! In natural families, the richer members often give some financial support to the poorer, though this can by no means be guaranteed (we all know the sort of bickering that can occur even in the best-regulated of families). But, as far as Paul was concerned, the sort of love shown in God's family should far outstrip this. Didn't Jesus say that the quality of Christians's love for one another would be a sign of their true discipleship? 'By this all men will know that you are my disciples, if you love one another' (John 13.35).

How can we capture that 'family' quality of loving and committed relationships in the church? This question is posed afresh to every generation of Christians. Often, the solution is seen as some form of Christian community living. The argument goes that if Christians are really serious about sharing their lives with one another, and expressing the *koinonia* of the Holy Spirit, they will want to adopt quite a radical lifestyle. Many attempts along these lines were made in the USA in the 1960s, influenced probably by the Hippy movement of that decade, and the growing disillusionment with materialism and affluent middle-class standards. I personally found these ideas attractive, and decided to investigate some of the American communities personally. After listening spellbound to Michael Harper's account of a visit to the Church of the Redeemer in Houston, Texas, and then devouring his book on the subject,[4] I embarked, in 1974, on a fact-finding tour of some of the USA Christian communities, including the one in Edinboro that I have already described.

After my visit there, I flew down to Houston to see the

Anglican Church of the Redeemer. Much was written about this church in the early 1970s, [5] it had a profound impact on renewal in this country, due mainly to the ministry of the Fisherfolk, the music group originating from that church, who sent a resident team to England at about that time. Although I had read the books, I decided that this was no substitute for seeing for myself. Redeemer was not an interdenominational community, but rather a local denominational church that had developed a community lifestyle. At the time when I visited, about half the congregation were living in community 'households'. As with the Edinboro community, it tended to be younger, single people who lived in this way, but there was also a substantial number of older, more mature Christians. The households were often led by a married couple with children, and sometimes contained other families as well as single people. Just as in Edinboro, large households of ten to twelve people, sleeping in bunk beds in shared rooms, were the order of the day. Incomes too were shared, and, as a result, an even higher proportion of people seemed to be working full-time for the church in such ministries as remodelling houses, maintaining buildings, servicing cars, running a multi-racial playgroup and administering the Fisherfolk's outreach. One difference between Redeemer and Edinboro was that Redeemer seemed to be using their households to minister to those with very deep needs, whereas at Edinboro the households did this to a lesser extent, but concentrated instead on being centres of discipleship and alternative Christian lifestyle.

These were the two communities where I spent the most time during a visit to the USA of nearly six weeks. They were representative of literally dozens which were flourishing there at that time. On the basis of my brief experience, I was able to assess some of the positives and negatives of this radical attempt to live according to the spirit of Acts chapter 2, verses 42 to 47.

Looking first at the positive side, there was clearly a sacrificial commitment to God, particularly in terms of communal worship and Bible-study. In a household this normally took place early, before going to work. There was also a nearly 100 per cent attendance from household members at all major church meetings. There was a similar depth of commitment to each other, first in actually being prepared to live in community, then in pooling incomes, sharing domestic chores and the care of children, and generally meeting one another's needs. There was an opportunity for some deep ministry to those with psychological and spiritual hurts, as well as to the socially deprived (e.g., the delinquent boys I have mentioned). New Christians could be helped and discipled by older ones.

As I have already noted, this way of living enabled many people to work full-time for the church. This is very helpful if the church has a large plant and a variety of ministries to maintain, as well as a lot of needy individuals who need jobs which often amount to a sort of 'occupational therapy' in a protected environment. Depth of commitment to one another encouraged a high degree of faith for God to move supernaturally, e.g. in simple examples of answered prayer, as well as in healings. At Redeemer, members were encouraged to 'share' publicly testimonies of how God had answered prayer in all sorts of ways – including even a small boy saying how God had provided him with a bicycle.

However, some aspects of the community lifestyle seemed to me less helpful. Personal prayer and Bible-study could get squeezed out by the emphasis laid on relating to one another. Also, there wasn't enough privacy. It was impossible to be in a room on one's own. Indeed, in my household at Redeemer this was positively discouraged as 'hiding away'.

At its worst, the style of leadership in the households could be authoritarian. This was no doubt partly because some of the household members were rather immature people who needed a strong, 'parental' style of guidance, with responsibilities taken off them. Unfortunately, however, this style of leadership could be extended to everyone. For example, in the household where I stayed at Redeemer, I was scolded (even as a guest!)

for not letting the leader know that I was going out to an ice-cream parlour one evening to talk with someone from another household. This reminded me of certain negative features of my boarding-school education, which I did not enjoy experiencing again at the age of 30!

More serious even than this was the real danger of marriage and the family unit being eroded. If too much emphasis is put on the fact that we are all brothers and sisters in Christ, then my wife very easily becomes 'the sister that I sleep with'. I was conscious too of a policy that only the household leaders had the right to discipline the children in their household. This meant that other couples with children had that right (which the Bible sees as a parent's duty – Eph. 6.4; I Tim. 3.4–5) taken away.

I returned from that visit admiring much of what I had experienced of the lifestyle of these Christian communities. In particular, the young household where I stayed in Edinboro struck me as being rather like my idea of the original Franciscan community, with an infectious sense of joy and brotherly love. On the other hand, Redeemer, a much more mature and varied group of Christians, seemed to be developing in a rather legalistic direction. It seems that an authentic move of the spirit towards a community lifestyle can quickly become authoritarian if the rights and responsibilities of each individual Christian before God are not stressed enough. The vertical relationship is always more basic and important than the horizontal.

If we lose that truth, the church becomes a club of like-minded people who are doing their best to help one another in a way that probably seems strange and excessive to the outside world. Church history has several examples of churches with a strong sense of community, which in time become very inward-looking and unusual. For example, some of the Amish, Mennonite Christians of North America, are organised in wonderfully supportive communities; but they go round in horse-drawn buggies, wear old-fashioned clothes, and have very little to do with the outside world, which they regard as being of the devil. Interestingly, the Christians at Redeemer seem to have realised the dangers of the path that they were treading. A friend of mine who visited the church five years later reported that almost all the community households had been disbanded, and that people were trying to express fellowship in less radical but possibly more appropriate ways.

Many of those communities in the USA, like the one at Edinboro, called themselves 'covenant communities'. The reason for that was that each member had to enter into a covenant with the other members to be more committed to them than to Christians outside the community. This would be quite normal in the monastic tradition. In most ages of the church since the early fourth century, there have been communities of Christians who have tried to live a disciplined life of devotion together. In monasticism, these have generally been single-sex, and have had a rule of celibacy along with rules of sharing possessions, and obedience to the leadership and discipline of the community. The Anabaptists at the Reformation also developed a community lifestyle, which can still be seen in such groups as the Hutterites today. They, too, have a particular covenant commitment to their community and its rule of life, though married couples and children are a vital part of the structure, and the marriage bond is honoured.

While I appreciate the fervour and vigour of covenant-style communities, it seems to me that there are two particular dangers inherent in them. The first applies also to traditional monasticism: that a Christian might regard membership of a covenant community as more important than his or her membership of the church. I once had a friend who was a Franciscan friar, and I remember how it used to grate on me whenever he referred to his 'brothers', i.e. his fellow-Franciscans. As far as I was concerned, I was just as much his brother in Christ as they were, whereas for him there was (understandably) a special relationship with them. He saw them as his family in a particular way.

There certainly is a depth and a commitment about covenant communities that exposes the superficiality of so-called 'fellowship' in the average church. But the New Testament says nothing about special communities within the wider church. In the early church, all relationships between Christians were special. The only covenant which bound church members together was the new covenant in the blood of Jesus. The early Christians were aware that Jesus' death had broken every barrier down and made them one (Eph. 2.14–6). It should be the same for us today. Any other covenant that Christians may make with one another may be helpful, but is much less important than this wonderful new covenant which God has established with us, and which joins us together as brothers and sisters.

The second danger is a down-grading of marriage. This can only occur in communities that include both married and single members. Marriage is itself a binding covenant entered into by husband and wife before God and human witnesses. Warmth of fellowship within a church always brings a stronger sense of the brother/sister relationships that we enjoy in God's family. But at the same time, we must always preserve the uniqueness of marriage. The Bible sees it as a very special expression of unity: 'For this reason a man will leave his father and mother and be united with his wife, and they will become one flesh' (Gen. 2.24). With the welcome sharing of responsibilities in the home which comes with community lifestyle, this uniqueness can become blurred. Also, in the intimacy of living under the same roof, obvious temptations can arise which can wreck a marriage if they are not recognised and strenuously resisted.

These problems don't just happen in communities. A classic situation, which might occur in any lively local church, but which is fraught with potential difficulties, is when a husband or wife starts ministering regularly with someone of the opposite sex who is not their marriage partner. For one thing, this looks strange to the outside world; non-Christians tend to jump to the worst possible conclusions, and Christians may be forgiven for doing the same! The real danger, however, is that an unhealthy relationship might develop. This doesn't have to be openly adulterous to be wrong. The strong emotional link that can so easily be formed will soon begin to undermine the marriage relationships involved. I remember hearing a mature and respected Christian counsellor describe how she had to stop counselling with a close male friend because she saw the potential dangers for her marriage. She now counsels exclusively with her husband. What a pity it is that more Christians don't have her wisdom and self-control! I know of highly gifted men and women whose ministries have been blighted and even brought to a halt by wrong relationships of this sort.

The best antidote to this danger is for husbands and wives as far as possible to develop joint ministries within the church. This is not always easy, if, for example, the wife has a gift of music and worship-leading, whereas the husband is tone-deaf but is an excellent administrator. But often there will be many areas where a married couple can minister together (perhaps, in the case above, the husband could administer the music group!)

Priscilla and Aquila are the great example in the early church of joint husband-and-wife ministry. First, we know that they had a gift of *hospitality*. They were the people who opened their home to Paul in Corinth (Acts 18.1–3), and it was they who invited Apollos into their home in Ephesus (Acts 18.26). They were the sort of couple who are a blessing in any local church, those who look out for visitors and make a point of inviting them round for coffee or lunch after the service. They also clearly had a ministry of *teaching and pastoral care*. It was they who nurtured the gifted convert Apollos, explaining to him more adequately what it meant to be a Christian (v.26). In fact, they were ideal home-group leaders, and it comes as no surprise that, no matter where they went in the Roman Empire, they always had a group of Christians meeting at their house (at Ephesus – I Cor. 16.19, and in Rome – Romans 16.3–5). Finally, they clearly had a *ministry to single people*. Paul and Apollos both benefitted from it. Many single people find it a joy to have a close friendship with a married couple, and to be welcomed into their family. I remember well how as a single person I greatly appreciated visiting my married friends, playing with their children, and being a part of their home for a while. It was like a breath of fresh air. In return, single people can be wonderful friends and supports to married couples (e.g. through baby-sitting), as we know only too well from our experience in our church.

As a married couple, my wife Val and I want to develop that sort of joint ministry as much as possible, and we are encouraging the other couples in our church to do the same. But if a married couple are to be effective together in Christian ministry in this way, they have to take certain positive steps to guard the unity of their relationship.

First, they need to *pray together*. Couples need to remember that it is God who has joined them together. He is the third strand of the 'threefold cord' of marriage (Eccles. 4.12). If he is in his rightful place, we can be sure that the cord will not easily be broken. Therefore we need regularly to come before God together in prayer. Many of us find that this is enormously difficult, either because we are embarrassed or because we don't seem to have the time. The only way to achieve it is to programme in a regular slot in the day. This may mean making a sacrifice; for example, at one time we found that, with three small children making almost constant demands on our time, it was only possible to pray together if we stopped watching the news on television. Even though we both enjoyed that particular news bulletin, we felt that praying together was more important – and we tried to catch up on the news at other times. As for the embarrassment factor, the only way to deal with this is to have the will to overcome it – and this only comes with perseverance and practice.

Then, they need to *spend time together*. This seems obvious, yet it is amazing how the time gets eroded. Once again, it is vital that time together gets programmed into the week. A married couple surely need at least one evening together a week, and many of us need more. These evenings need to be written into diaries; after that has been done, we have a 'previous engagement' for that evening which is certainly as important as a church meeting. If we have children, we also need to have definite 'family times' together, when we can go out and enjoy ourselves, or be at home and relax. If a family friend joins us, well and good, provided that it is understood that this isn't a time for intense pastoral conversations or for talking shop about our work.

Having set aside time together, couples need to use it to *communicate openly* with one another. We often find this surprisingly difficult. Husbands, in particular, seem to be out of touch with their own emotions, and have trouble expressing what they are feeling and thinking. Also, masculine pride often prevents them from admitting to needs and weaknesses. But if we truly allow the Holy Spirit into our marriage, he will start to sort us out. In the protected and special lifelong relationship of trust and openness that marriage alone truly is, we can begin to express our fears and negatives as well as our strengths, secure in the knowledge that we can work through the problems together.

Finally, they need to put into practice in marriage everything that the Bible teaches about *relationships in general*. For example, forgiveness needs to be worked out in the marriage; so does loving confrontation in a situation of conflict; and so does a serving attitude. It's a sobering thought that our neighbours will to a large extent judge our Christianity by the quality of our family life: the way we talk to and about one another, how we care for and discipline our children, and the noises that come through the party wall if we are having a row.

A local church should express as much as possible the real *koinonia* of the Holy Spirit without the non-scriptural excesses. It should be a community where various lifestyles are acceptable, both those who choose to live in extended families and those who don't. It should recognise the unique contribution that both single and married people have in God's family. No group within the church should be seen or see themselves as more spiritual or authentically 'biblical' in their expression of community than another. To end the chapter, let's look at some of the ways that Christians can express their family identity, most of which are mentioned in Acts chapter 2.

We can *spend time together* (Acts 2.44). It's good if we can keep as open a home as possible. This can be difficult, especially if we're coping with babies or battling with toddlers, and we must be careful not to put expectations on one another that are unrealistic. Each of us is very different, and it is loving and sensitive to learn how the other person functions. Other people 'dropping round' can be a problem if we're working to tight schedules when our children are in the pre-school years (I write with considerable experience, both of our own children and of the families in our church, whose children are mostly three and under). A sensitive use of the phone, even with close neighbours, can be a kind gesture before dropping round. Having said that, we do need to spend time together, in order to get to know each other, have fun with each other, and express what it means to be God's family. Churches which are geographically based have a distinct advantage here over the 'gathered congregation' whose members come from far and wide to worship at the church of their choice (though that problem can partly be solved by locally-based home-groups). This is the reason why most House Churches put such a strong emphasis on the locality where you live. This should be motivated not by a heavy authoritarianism ('If you want to join us you must move to our neighbourhood'), but by a desire for church members to enjoy as much fellowship and mutual support as possible. This will be a great witness in the neighbourhood, especially as the church's influence spills over into non-Christian homes.

Obviously, it's much easier for wives who don't go out to work to spend time together than for any other section of the church. Opportunities need to be created for the others. Men in particular find it difficult to unwind and get to know one another in a relaxed way. In our church we have had special get-togethers for men which have proved quite successful. Sometimes they've taken the form of discussions (on such topics as 'being a Christian at work' or even 'the meaning of masculinity for a Christian'!), at other times they've been purely social. We also have evenings when the women get together and the men babysit.

We can, to some extent at least, *have things in common* (Acts 2.44). We need to learn how to share our possessions. I remember how impressed and touched I was the first time another Christian offered to lend me his car any time I wanted it. He wasn't even someone I knew very well. Those of us who have lived in community know both the joy of sharing possessions and the irritation of finding that something that is 'ours' has been misused. We need to learn two things before we start sharing possessions: first, that we are simply stewards of the things God has given us, and second, that we need to respect other people's stewardship when we borrow their things. It's very disheartening to receive back a blunt chisel or a cracked vase, especially when there's no apology or offer to make good the damage. In our church, a great deal of sharing goes on, but we certainly haven't arrived at the warm openness of the Jerusalem church. This will only come through a deep work of the Holy Spirit in our hearts.

We also need to learn to *share our food and our homes* (Acts 2.46). Mutual hospitality is a great way of saying that we love and care for one another. I believe that we shouldn't just entertain our close personal friends, but ask God regularly who *he* wants us to have to meals. Entertaining is much more exciting and rewarding that way. It's also very enjoyable to express our unity as a church by regularly all having large meals together when everyone brings a contribution. Some of us will also feel called to have other members of the church to live with us. Such arrangements should never be entered into lightly, and we should feel God's call to live in this way. Singles will probably already be sharing flats (or increasingly, houses), and they too will have to find ways of expressing community and maintaining the unity of their households.

Finally, we can share in *prayer, Bible-study and Holy Communion* (Acts 2.42). Many churches nowadays are organised into 'home groups' or 'house groups', consisting of between ten and twenty church members who all live in the same locality. These groups are a way of expressing the family aspect of the church in all its different dimensions. They can have a purely social function; having meals together, or playing silly games, for example. More usually, the meeting would consist of a time of worship, followed by prayer for matters of shared concern, and ministry to group members who are in need. This could be followed by group Bible-study, with emphasis on the participation of every member, and a simple, informal form of Holy Communion (with or without an ordained minister present, depending on your theology).

What goes on in between group meetings is obviously very important. A group whose members only meet once a week won't be a very effective means of expressing their family unity in Christ. The members need to make time for one another in between meetings, so that barriers can be broken down and friendships formed. Members of the group, especially the leaders, will have a pastoral concern for one another, which takes the pressure off the full-time pastors. But it is also very important, and good for healthy relationships, if the group has an outward focus in evangelism and 'Jesus action' in the community. Door-to-door visiting, or decorating someone's house together, can be a wonderful means of drawing the group together.

Each local church needs to find ways of expressing family unity that are appropriate for it. We don't all have to live under the same roof and sleep in bunk beds to know the reality of Christian community. However we do it, though, one thing is vital: our expression of community must be one which embraces the outsider. We must not be so turned in on ourselves, our personal friendships and parochial preoccupations that the Christian visitor, the new convert, or the non-Christian who has wandered in feels excluded, unwelcome and unloved. Also, we should not want to cling on to church members who feel that God is calling them to change churches within our locality or move to a new job in another place. There should be no constraint in the family of God except that of God's love. It is always sad to see Christian brothers and sisters, close friends perhaps, leave but they are still part of the family, wherever they go. For this family is not bound by time or space, as we shall realise fully one day when we enjoy a great reunion in heaven.

PART III

Where We're At

Chapter 7

Why Denominations?

Having looked at unity on a small scale, both in the relationship of the individual with God and in relationships within the local church, we can now turn to the larger dimension, *unity between churches*. First, we need to look at the concept and history of *denominations*. When we think about Christian unity in this country (and, I suspect, generally around the world), we don't think so much about what the Bible says about unity as about the unity of denominations. The danger of this is that instead of facing up to the real problems of unity, we are tackling ones that are secondary or even irrelevant. If what I have argued in the previous chapters is true, it is impossible for two denominations to think that they can 'unite' simply by joining together organisationally, accepting one another's ministries and encompassing one another's theology. On the one hand, true unity in the Holy Spirit is such a profound thing that it can simply short-circuit denominational divides. On the other, no amount of discussion or making covenants with other denominations can achieve unity if there is not the authentic 'unity of heart and soul'. However, there is no doubt that denominations and a denominational way of thinking represent a serious obstacle to unity. We therefore need, at this point, to look at denominations: how they come about, what they are, and how they can unite to form new structures.

Let's first try to define 'denomination'. Interestingly, the word is one which most denominations avoid like the plague! It doesn't, for example, appear as an entry in the *Oxford Dictionary of the Christian Church*. We prefer to describe our particular ecclesiastical structure as a 'church'. But that is not a biblical definition of 'church'. In the New Testament, 'church' is used either (1) of the universal church (e.g. Col. 1.18, 'He is the head of the body, the church'), or (2) of the church in a particular city (e.g. II Cor. 1.1,' To the church of God in Corinth'), or (3) of what we would call a 'house group' or 'home group' (e.g. I Cor. 16.19, 'Aquila and Priscilla greet you warmly in the Lord, and so does the church that meets at their house').

The word 'church' itself is a translation of the Greek *ekklesia*, meaning an *assembly*, and was used by the early Christians to describe those that had been called by the Lord to meet together. My favourite definition of 'church' occurs in the *Book of Common Prayer*. In the second (alternative) prayer after communion in the service of Holy Communion, the church is described as *'the blessed company of all faithful people'*. I find this a wonderfully clear and all-embracing definition. It includes every true believer in Christ, no matter what their denomination. It also emphasises, rightly to my mind, that the genuine church is defined by faith rather than by participation. In other words, it is possible to be a member of a church, to attend regularly, and to take part in all church activities, without truly being a member of the body of Christ. For that, you must have a personal faith in Christ, and be living out that faith in reality.

So what is a denomination, if it isn't a biblical definition of 'church'? Historically, it has to do with the church splitting. In my understanding, a denomination is a grouping of Christian churches which is defined not so much by geography as by a particular doctrinal or theological interpretation of biblical truth. For that reason, a denomination is always a partial, incomplete Christian structure, and can in no way claim to be the 'one, holy, catholic and apostolic church'.

It might be helpful here if I sketch out a history of the rise of denominations.[1] It will have to be brief and superficial. I am assuming no previous knowledge at all on the part of the reader! It might appear at first sight that the church remained relatively united for about 1,000 years. During that long period, however, many groups split off from the main (or *Catholic*) body of the church, and some of these continued for several centuries. For example, the *Montanists* in the second century were a prophetic group (today they would be called 'charismatic') dedicated to holiness and rigorous self-discipline. Named after their leader, Montanus, they were condemned by the Catholic bishops, but Montanist churches continued for another 300 years. On the other hand, the third-century *Novatianists,* based at first in Rome, were totally orthodox. They differed from the Catholics only in refusing to receive back those who had renounced Christ under persecution. They set up a network of small congregations, and were treated as heretics until the fourth century, when the Christian Emperor Constantine granted them toleration. Finally the *Donatists* in the fourth century were a North African phenomenon. Named after Donatus, their bishop in Carthage, they similarly stood for holiness and steadfastness in the face of persecution by the Roman emperors. They were then persecuted by the Catholic church for having too rigorous an attitude in refusing to accept back into fellowship believers who apostatised under persecution. Nevertheless, they survived in North Africa until the seventh century. These are just three examples of fairly orthodox groups that were persecuted by their fellow-Christians, partly at any rate for being too spiritual or rigorous. They are representative of the 'denominations' of the early church.

Some schismatic groups, on the other hand, were clearly heretical. In the first three centuries of the church, the heresies centred around the nature of Jesus: how far was he human, how far divine, and how were his humanity and divinity related? Some groups overstressed his humanity, others his divinity, while the position that finally won the day as orthodox trod a fine line down the middle. Once that position was clearly established, it became the norm for the church, and was adopted into the creeds which formed the basis of the faith, most notably the creed of the church council of Chalcedon (AD 451).

One large group of Christians with slightly unorthodox views came into being just after Chalcedon. They were the *Monophysites,* who taught that there was a single, divine nature in the human body of the incarnate Christ as opposed to the orthodox teaching of a double nature, divine and human. The difference between this and the orthodox position is subtle, and the Catholics made various attempts to woo the Monophysites back during the fifth and sixth centuries. When these failed, the latter formed themselves into three great groupings: the Copts/Ethiopians, the Syrians and the Armenians. These churches are still very much in existence, distinct both from each other and from Roman Catholic and Orthodox churches. They cannot be called non-Christian, as their theology is in almost every respect completely orthodox. The Copts in Egypt in particular have been experiencing revival in recent years, and have seen considerable growth as well as persecution. They are clearly separate denominations, each one with a strongly national flavour, and with ancient traditions and ways of worship.

However, the biggest split in the church's history before the Reformation of the sixteenth century was between the *Eastern and Western parts of the Catholic church* in 1054. This break was, in fact, the result of centuries of separate development, with a long history of disagreement on minor matters such as the way the two parts of the church worshipped, how they were administered, and their slightly differing versions of the Creed. The Crusades brought the two halves of Christendom closer, as armies from Western Europe swept through Byzantium on the way to the Holy Land to liberate Jerusalem from Islamic control, but this did not make for an easier relationship. The Pope, the Bishop of Rome, wanted to control Christendom, but the Patriarch of Constantinople, the second most powerful bishop, would have none of it. In this way, a combination of political and ecclesiastical factors made the split inevitable. Sadly, each side excommunicated the other. Since that time, even the Catholic church has been divided into two groupings, the *Western* churches under the authority of Rome (which include some so-called 'eastern rite' churches who retain Eastern ways of worship), and those outside it (the majority of *Orthodox* churches), under the authority of various Patriarchs (senior archbishops). According to my definition, these two groupings are clearly denominational. Although a new era of friendship and co-operation between them was clearly established at the Second Vatican Council (1963–5), and the mutual excommunications were lifted in 1965, they have not so far united.

I have gone into these historical details to try to show that denominations existed before the sixteenth century, since some people pin all the blame for denominations on the Reformation. I also wanted to show that at least some of these early denominations represented a purer, more rigorous form of Christianity than that of the official, Catholic church.

Certainly, it was the *Reformation* which marked the next great split in the church, this time within Western Christendom. Clearly, Protestantism has within itself seeds of schism. There is a tendency in the Protestant mentality to want to split, and this arises from a desire (sometimes courageous and commendable, sometimes downright wrongheaded) to make a stand on points of doctrine. When Luther nailed his ninety-five theses to the door of the Schlosskirche in Wittenberg in 1517, he was making some very clear theological statements that ran contrary to the theology and practice of Western Catholicism (i.e. of Rome) at that time.

But the name 'Protestant' originated from a formal 'protest' made by six princes and fourteen cities to the Archduke Ferdinand of Austria defending freedom of conscience and the right of minorities. As so often happens in the affairs of the church, there was an alliance of religion and politics. The strong religious conviction of the reformers happened to coincide with the political aspirations of the German princes. This alliance was nowhere more apparent than in the formation of the Church of England, where, in the words of James Atkinson, 'the Reformation, though religious in origin, became entangled with politics by corrupt and scheming men concerned only to do well for themselves in a turbulent situation.'[2] Yet although Henry VIII's break with Rome came clearly because the Pope would not sanction the King's proposed divorce of Queen Catherine, he had in Thomas Cranmer a great reforming Archbishop of Canterbury, who went on to introduce the ideas of the Reformation considerably more effectively during the short reign of Edward VI (1547–53).

The Reformation gave rise to a number of denominations. Some, like the *Lutherans, Reformed* (or *Presbyterian*) churches, and *Anglicans*, have grown extremely large. Originally established as the national church in the various countries in Europe where they were encouraged to flourish by political leaders, they have now become vast worldwide denominations, partly because of the missionaries they have sent out during the last 200 years, and partly because of the political colonies established overseas by the nations whose official state church they were. Other denominations, like the *Mennonites* and *Moravians*, were more radical in their reforms than the others, and as a result were persecuted by both Catholics and Protestants. Despite this, they still exist, and though not large by comparison, have a worldwide membership of more than 600,000.

In the 450 years since the Reformation, countless other denominations have formed. The *Congregationalists* developed in the late sixteenth century in reaction against the Church of England, which they regarded as not reformed enough. They believed in the autonomy of the local congregation, and set up an independent congregation of their own. For this they were imprisoned and harassed by the government. Some of their leaders fled abroad, and it was one of these who started the *Baptist* movement. Now the largest denomination worldwide after Roman Catholicism, the Baptists' particular theological emphasis was on adult or 'believer's' baptism, and they too sought freedom from state interference.

The next major denomination to emerge in England was *Methodism*. This resulted from a movement of evangelical revival led by John Wesley and George Whitefield in the eighteenth century. At a time of great spiritual dryness and moral laxity in the Church of England, these leaders emphasised the necessity of personal conversion and moral purity. Travelling preachers toured the country on horseback speaking to thousands in the open air. As a result, many were converted, and the nation experienced a remarkable spiritual 'awakening'. In order to nurture the converts, Wesley devised an efficient organisation or 'society'. He did not intend to found a denomination separate from the Church of England (of which he was an ordained minister), but rather a fellowship within it. He assumed that his converts would become good Anglicans, and he had no desire to leave the established church. Unfortunately, however, this revival was opposed by the majority of the bishops of the Church of England, and after Wesley's death, Methodism became in effect a separate denomination, and is now established as such worldwide.

Since the eighteenth century, Protestant denominations have continued to proliferate. Most have based themselves on a particular theological interpretation of the Scriptures: for example, Methodism split early on into the 'Arminian' and 'Calvinistic' Methodists, who differed on their doctrine of salvation. Although the Methodists in England are now united after a number of splits over the years, there still remains a separate group of Calvinist Methodists in Wales. Important and influential denominations to arise in the nineteenth century include the *Christian Brethren* (also known as *Open Brethren*) and the *Salvation Army*, each with its own characteristic emphasis.

The twentieth century has seen more denominations arise than any other. Undoubtedly, the most significant denominational grouping to emerge has been *Pentecostalism*. In fact, James Dunn considers that this represents 'a fourth major strand of Christianity – alongside Orthodoxy, Roman Catholicism and Protestantism'.[3] Pentecostalism, an offshoot of evangelical Protestantism,

99

is based on a rediscovery of the person, work and manifestations of the Holy Spirit. The particular sign that gave rise to the movement was the gift of 'speaking in tongues', i.e. praying to God in a language unknown to the speaker. Pentecostalism arose almost simultaneously in the USA, England and Sweden in the early years of the century, and has since swept around the world. By far the fastest-growing sector of the church, it has a strong emotional and experiential element, and appeals particularly to Third-World Christians with little formal education. Pentecostalism has also rediscovered the miraculous element in a gospel which Western theologians had almost completely 'demythologised'. Healings and other miracles feature large in its church life and evangelism.

One unfortunate feature of Pentecostalism is that it seems to be particularly prone to denominationalism. This may be because ethnic Pentecostal churches often centre around strong and gifted leaders who are not always good at working with those who have a slightly different vision. It has also aroused a great deal of animosity among more traditional evangelical Christians because of its emphasis on the miraculous and its theology of a 'second blessing' of the Holy Spirit subsequent to conversion. The Pentecostal pioneers were condemned by many other evangelicals as being 'of the devil', and this sort of suspicion seems to have stuck, although in most respects Pentecostal and evangelical theology are identical.

Yet another important characteristic of Pentecostalism has been its ability to influence the older denominations. In the so-called *Charismatic Renewal*, first (in the 1950s) the Protestants, then (in the 1960s) the Roman Catholics and some Orthodox, and finally (in the 1980s) even some of the hostile evangelicals have been revitalised or 'renewed' by the experiential element of Pentecostalism. As I described in Chapter 2, I myself experienced this in the unexpected academic surroundings of Cambridge University. Undoubtedly, this shared experience of the reality of Christ through the power and love of the Holy

Spirit can have the effect of drawing together Christians of widely differing denominations and traditions in an unusually powerful way. One example of this is the way that the leading Anglican evangelical and charismatic David Watson could feel so drawn to 'renewed' Roman Catholics that he could say publicly to an audience of fellow-evangelicals that the Reformation was 'one of the greatest tragedies that ever happened to the church'[4] – a courageous, controversial remark which by no means endeared him to everyone.

The Church in England today contains most of the denominations described above, with the addition of one important new grouping: the *House Churches*.[5] The name arose in the 1960s when Christians who had left denominational churches started to meet in private houses. In fact, many House Churches are now so large (some have over 1,000 members in a local church) that they have to meet in hired halls. Others have purchased large buildings, such as redundant cinemas, and remodelled them to suit their needs. From the first, House Church teaching has been strongly 'anti-denominational', but ironically they have quickly developed quasi-denominational structures. As they have usually emphasised the ministry of contemporary 'apostles' in the church, they have urged local groups to affiliate together under the leadership or 'covering' of one of their recognised 'apostles'. Bryn Jones, Terry Virgo and John Noble are all men who are regarded as such by a number of churches which they lead.

House Church theology has tended to be very suspicious of historic denominations, which have been regarded as spiritually dry, 'old wineskins' which cannot hold the new wine of the Holy Spirit. Strongly charismatic, they have found the structures and traditions of historic Pentecostalism too restricting, and have responded with new music, fervent praise and dancing in worship; a high expectation of the miraculous; and, recently, a lively interest in evangelism and church growth. One very positive development is that, within the first generation of House Churches, their leaders are beginning to respond in a warm and brotherly fashion to those very denominations they reacted against and left. It remains to be seen where this will lead. In the meantime, House Church hymns and songs continue to pour out, finding their way into the worship of every other denomination, and the evangelistic thrust of such churches as Ichthus Christian Fellowship in 'z South London and Clarendon Church in Brighton set the pace for most other churches in the nation.

Denominationalism has built into it certain negative characteristics. A denomination tends, at the very least, to be *critical* of other denominations. This is basically because of entrenched theological differences, but, as we have seen, rational criticism can easily escalate to the irrational lengths of damning other Christians as satanic, and even of accusing them of various immoral practices. To the shame of the church, criticism can also develop into outright persecution. This has happened in the most gruesome way at some periods of church history, with the Inquisition (though by the standards of the day a very fair court) a permanent historical reminder of how sinful Christians can be in the way that they have been prepared to torture and kill each other. Protestants, too, have atrocities to answer for, e.g. the Roman Catholic martyrs during the reign of Elizabeth I. We can thank God that in this century, such gross persecution of Christians by Christians has ceased, though it is still possible in Western Europe for evangelicals to face criminal charges for preaching the Gospel to a member of another denomination which happens to be a state church (this occurred recently in Greece). Normally nowadays, persecution between denominations takes more subtle forms: barbed remarks, personal attacks in print, and things of that sort.

Denominations have a tendency to be *separatist*, retreating into their own particular ghetto. In England today, the Church of England, being the established church, is not so prone to this, but sometimes has an effortless sense of its own superiority which can be irritating (or so I have observed from the reactions of some of my Free Church friends). The smaller Free Churches have tended to be very caught up in their own organisations, while the more radically independent groups have 'done their own thing' without reference to anyone else, particularly if they have a strong doctrinal axe to grind. The Roman Catholics, almost as numerous as the Anglicans, also relate very largely within their own structures. Of course, there are those within each denomination who make a determined effort to cross the boundaries and meet each other. These are the fully paid-up 'ecumaniacs', but they represent only a small proportion of the total membership of each church.

It is also very easy for one denomination to slip into a *competitive* way of thinking and behaving. This is particularly the case in evangelism, and can cause real confusion in an unevangelised country where a number of denominations move their missionaries in and start fishing for souls. Each denomination, being made up of sinful human beings, feels that their particular approach is the best, so the denominations become in effect competing brands of Christianity. On a more local level, this sort of competition can also occur between churches of the same denomination, e.g. Anglican churches with differing theologies. Also, awkward situations can arise where Christians move from one local church to another (of the same or a different denomination), giving rise to accusations of 'sheep-stealing'. For unity in love to be maintained between local churches, everything depends on the graciousness with which these situations are handled by the parties concerned.

If these three negative features of denominationalism are to be avoided, we need to put into practice the three attitudes which provide an antidote in each case. These are, first, a determination to be *encouraging*. We need to be positive and upbuilding in what we say to members of another denomination, and about that denomination. We need to be prepared to grant, at the very least, that some of the its members might *just* be Christians! We should also be very careful what we say behind their backs, and we need to pray for them. Even as I write,

I am conscious that there is a local clergyman for whom I have never prayed; mentally, I have written him off. How true would that be of you? If we are praying for someone, we are more likely to think and speak well of him. I know that I have a tendency to praise with faint damns, and I know that this is a real weakness among Christians when talking about one another's churches. How many times have you heard a comment like, 'Oh yes, St Botolph's is very good on evangelism. A pity that their pastoral network is so poor'? How often have you made such a comment? We find it very difficult to speak out what is positive and omit to mention the negative. Yet the New Testament reminds us that 'love covers a multitude of sins' (I Peter 4.8). We might be more careful in our comments, too, if we applied to ourselves the same standards that we expect of other Christians when they speak of us and our church.

Next, we should be prepared to *communicate openly* with members of other denominations. If we are church leaders, we should make an effort to go to the ministers' fraternal. However tedious it may be at times (it often isn't!), we need to have enough self-confidence to know that it would be far worse without us. We should be prepared to listen, ask questions, look ignorant, and be vulnerable to others' probing questions. I have been put through the mangle on several occasions by brother clergy who don't approve of what I'm doing. I have learnt that they have usually been misinformed, and that when they hear the facts they become much more gracious and accepting. I have learnt too that to step outside mainstream denominational life, as I have done, can pose quite a threat to leaders of more traditional churches. But whether people are accepting or not, I am learning to take the flak meekly, knowing that in doing so I am sharing in the vulnerability of Christ himself. Any Christian could find himself in a similar position. We can either react self-protectively or with an openness that is in fact the only way to a greater depth of reality.

Finally, we need to learn *humility*. Deep in the heart

of denominationalism is the sin of pride. We are usually convinced that our way is the best. This is particularly the case if we have moved from one denomination to another. In our search for unity, we all need to come to the place where we can sincerely repent of our feeling of superiority. We need to realise that however correct our doctrine is, we have often missed out on the love of God; however exciting our worship is, we have sometimes been too noisy to hear him speak; however many miracles we have seen or done, we are usually far from holy; however perfect our liturgy, our lives are often empty and fruitless. The churches that will find their humility tested to the utmost are those that really are getting somewhere spiritually. We all have to learn that we haven't really got very far unless the humility of Jesus has been worked into the fabric of our lives. It is not easy for us to admit that we need each other, but the Lord will not be satisfied with anything less than perfect fellowship in the Holy Spirit.

There is also, it must be said, a *positive* side to denominations (not to denominational*ism* which is a narrowly denominal way of thinking). A denomination enshrines particular traditions of theology (thinking and speaking about God), of liturgy (ways of worship), of church order (structure and ministry), of evangelism, and of social action. We tend to be very ignorant about each other's ways of thinking and acting, and this leads to prejudice. We need to listen and learn so that each denomination can make its distinctive contribution to the universal and the local church.[6] To give a few obvious examples: Roman Catholics can teach us about the universality of the church, about historical continuity, about humility and submission to authority within the church, about Christian community, and about selfless and dedicated service to the poor and needy. The Orthodox bring a deep spirituality, an emphasis on the transcendence of God, and a rich liturgical tradition. The Church of England reminds us that we have a mission to the nation, and a pastoral and evangelistic responsibility which is local.

105

Presbyterians bring insights about the grace of God, and about eldership in the Church. Baptists contribute their understanding of baptism, while Methodists bring an emphasis on personal conversion and holiness, together with a social concern, along with the glorious hymns of Charles Wesley to enrich our worship. Pentecostals remind us of the supernatural gifts of the Holy Spirit, and the House Churches teach us lessons of commitment to one another and of zealous neighbourhood evangelism. These examples are just the tip of the iceberg, for each denomination brings the fruit of years of thought, worship and witness. True unity will never be uniformity, but will include the richness of different traditions.

We need to be clear, too, that God can renew churches of any denomination – and can indeed renew whole denominations if their members are open to him. I have heard 'renewed' Christians write off a church because it is Anglican or Methodist or even Penetecostal; but in fact God is working powerfully in all those denominations. It seems to me that all he is seeking are men and women with humble hearts who are prepared to acknowledge their need, cry out to him, and go along with anything he decides to do with them. As John Wimber often says, 'God is not an English gentleman'. He may do the unexpected in our midst, and turn our traditions upside down. But he hasn't written off any denomination, as far as I am aware.

What about the differences that divide the denominations? The most profound ones seem to be theological and structural. On the *theological* side, we need to distinguish between essential beliefs that all Christians need to profess, and the peripheral ones which can be the subject of debate. The most essential article of faith seems to be the recognition that Jesus Christ is Lord, and that God raised him from the dead: 'If you confess with your mouth, "Jesus is Lord", and believe in your heart that God raised him from the dead, you will be saved' (Romans 10.9). True faith also involves a personal commitment to Jesus as the Son of God

who on the cross paid the price for our sin so that
we might receive God's forgiveness. Yet even as I write
this sentence, I am aware that I am making a theological
statement which is inadequate. The Scriptures speak of
Christ's death and its meaning with such a rich variety
of language and symbolism that one credal statement is
quite inadequate to capture its significance. So I would
agree with David Watson when he wrote, 'The doctrinal
basis for unity must be the unchangeable Gospel of
Jesus Christ, as given in the Scriptures as a whole.'[7]
Christians need to accept the Bible as the only basis
of doctrine and, indeed, of practice. I know that this
begs various questions. One is, *'which Scriptures?'*. The
Roman Catholic, Orthodox and Monophysite churches
accept books as scriptural which the Protestant churches
do not. Yet at any rate they do include in their Bibles
the whole content of the Protestant Scriptures. Even
more important is the question of *interpretation*. We
may agree on what is scriptural, but we certainly do
not agree on how to expound it. Yet at least we have a
common scriptural starting-point, and that is vital once
we start to discuss specific doctrinal difficulties. Some of
the thorniest of these will be examined in more detail in
Chapter 9.

As far as church *structure* is concerned, we need to
accept that the various patterns that have emerged over
the centuries can all be said to have some biblical basis.
We need in particular to be able to accept each other's
individuality and right to be different. We need also to
see that the way forward to unity is not for a smaller
denomination to be sucked into a larger one, and so lose
its individuality, but for us to be open to the Spirit of
God to create entirely new patterns in the future, which
are more appropriate to the new situation.

The twentieth century has been remarkable, not
simply for the rise of lots more denominations, but
also for a great movement for denominational unity.
Known as the 'Ecumenical Movement' (*oikumene* is the
Greek word for 'the inhabited earth'), it arose from
a desire among the non-Roman churches to show

a united face to the world in mission. In 1910, at about the same time that Pentecostalism was born, an International Missionary Conference took place in Edinburgh. 'Its task was to survey the world mission of the non-Roman churches. Over 1,000 delegates from all over the world encountered each other across the denominational divides.'[8] Three strands emerged from this conference: the International Missionary Council, to co-ordinate the missionary work of the denominations; the 'Faith and Order' movement, to discuss the doctrinal questions that divided the denominations; and 'Life and Work', to explore ways in which they could unite in service to the world. In 1948, the second two of these three strands united as the 'World Council of Churches' (WCC), with its headquarters in Geneva, to be joined by the IMC in 1961. Also in that year, the Orthodox churches were represented at a full assembly of the council, as were some Pentecostal churches.

The Roman Catholic church has never been a member of the WCC, although it has sent 'participating observers' to more recent full assemblies. The second half of this century has, however, seen the most remarkable revolution in its own ways of thinking, which has in turn led it to a greater openness in dialogue with other denominations. Pope John XXIII threw wide the windows of the Roman Catholic church to the Holy Spirit when he called the Second Vatican Council (1962–5). Out of this has come much greater dialogue with denominations, some doctrinal agreement (e.g. with the Anglicans), and even a degree of intercommunion with the Orthodox. Colin Buchanan comments, 'The emergence of the Church of Rome as a partner in ecumenical discussions . . . has totally changed ecumenical relationships'.[9]

I do not want to try to assess the merits and defects of the Ecumenical Movement. I believe that it was originally inspired by God, and that God can and does still use it, in so far as the participating churches stay close to him and to the Scriptures. I am, however, disturbed by some of the theology that emanates from the WCC in Geneva, as it seems to emphasise the political dimensions of the Gospel out of all proportion.

Denominations are the result of complex historical processes. They are a 'given' of the ecclesiastical situation, and although they do not correspond in any way to the biblical definition of 'church', we have to accommodate them in our thinking about unity. True unity will never be attained by mere structural unity, but the World Council of Churches presents, at the very least, an opportunity for dialogue and debate between the member churches, which may result in greater unity of heart.

Chapter 8

The National Scene

Having looked at the rise of denominations, and the international dimension of the ecumenical movement, we can now turn to some of the organisations and forces that operate *nationally* to give a lead in drawing Christians together. Readers from other nations will have to face different circumstances – and problems. In some countries, the Christian landscape is dominated by one denomination (e.g. the Roman Catholic church in most southern European nations, the Lutheran church in Sweden, the Orthodox church in Greece), leaving the other churches often feeling defensive and beleagured. There may even be a legacy of persecution of one denomination by another. In other countries, notably the USA, there is such a maze of denominations that the search for unity becomes extremely complex. Even among evangelicals there exists a bewildering variety of doctrinal points of view, so that, for example, one's view about the 'Rapture' becomes a touchstone of orthodoxy.

In contrast with these situations, the UK scene is characterised by an interesting balance between the denominations. Roughly, 30 per cent of all practising Christians are Anglican (Episcopalian), 30 per cent are Roman Catholic, and the remaining 40 per cent consists of the other Protestant churches. In England, taken alone, the balance is slightly different, with the Anglicans representing 40 per cent, the Roman Catholic 30 per cent, and the remaining Protestant churches 30 per cent. The latter are fairly clearly defined: the largest denominations are Methodist, United Reformed (a union of Presbyterian and Congregationalist), Baptist, Pentecostal, Brethren, House-Church, and the black-led churches. I should also mention the Orthodox churches, which are comparatively small, but rapidly increasing.[1]

The main body seeking to help unite Christians from

all these denominations is the *British Council of Churches* (BCC). Its membership includes most of the established denominations, apart from the Roman Catholics and the Pentecostals, but it is in the middle of a process of change which will radically transform it. Other bodies also draw Christians together, but because of their theological or moral stance are more likely than the BCC to exclude others. The *Evangelical Alliance* specifically aims to unite and be the voice of the wide-ranging evangelical constituency. Its members include both individuals and individual churches, but not denominations. Finally, national issues like the *Sunday Trading Bill* and David Alton's *Abortion (Amendment) Bill* draw all sorts of Christians together. We shall look at these in turn.

Local councils of churches in England had started to form as early as the First World War in the aftermath of the Edinburgh Conference of 1910 (see Chapter 7). The formation of the BCC in 1942 provided a body to co-ordinate these councils and also a stimulus for the formation of many more. By 1960 there were 650, and this number has remained fairly constant since. The BCC has given a lead to its member-churches in fields such as international and social questions, youth, evangelism, faith, and church order. Concern for refugees and the Third World led to the expansion of the BCC divisions into Christian Aid (the first Christian Aid Week was held in 1957). The Week of Prayer for Christian Unity developed over these years, and has provided an opportunity for Christians to pray for one another and to worship together. The BCC has also initiated inter-church study projects intended to draw together Christians from different local churches (e.g. 'People Next Door' in 1967).

Since January 1984, the BCC has been involved in what it calls an 'Inter-Church Process', a radical rethink of its aims, priorities and structures. This has been and still is a deep and searching pilgrimage for the church representatives involved, and when it is completed (in September 1990) it will provide a very different context for the quest for Christian unity at a national level. By that time, the BCC will have ceased to exist, and been replaced by new bodies for England, Wales, Scotland, and an overall co-ordinating body responsible for the UK and Ireland.

The 'Process', entitled 'Not Strangers but Pilgrims', has centred around a fundamental question: 'In your tradition and experience, how do you understand the nature and purpose of your church (or churches): 1) in relation to other Christian denominations; and 2) as together we share in God's mission to the world?' This question was considered and answered in three phases.

The first of these, from 1985–6, involved the different ways that various denominations understood the concept of 'church'. At local level, there was an inter-church Lent course based on a study-book called *What on Earth is the Church for?* The Archbishop of Canterbury commented, 'Instead of the hierarchies passing things down, this time we are trying it the proper way round – the local debate will be fed into the wider national reflection and discussion.'[2] About one million people took part in the discussions, and the programme was followed through fifty-seven radio stations as well as the group meetings. As a result, both the groups and 100,000 individual participants reported back. Ten per cent of the individual questionnaires were analysed. The opinions expressed represent the largest cross-section of views of British churchgoers ever available. They have been gathered and published in a book, *Views from the Pews*. The group reports in particular showed a deep longing, even a demand, for unity expressed by thousands of lay people.

At a national level, denominational churches were also invited to produce their own brief response to the question. Views of national bodies such as the EA were also invited. Over thirty churches are participating in 'Not Strangers But Pilgrims', and the responses of twenty-six of them have also been published in a second volume, *Reflections*. The list of these churches contains some surprises, including the Brethren alongside the Roman Catholics. It is good to see a representation from some of the black-led churches. The responses of some non-participating churches (including a House Church contribution from Philip Vogel), and other Christian bodies (including EA and the British Evangelical Council), together with some reflections on Third-World churches and international inter-denominational dialogue, is collected in a third book, *Observations*.[3] All this material makes interesting reading, but reflects very different views.

During the second phase, during autumn/winter 1986–7, inter-church meetings at all levels were encouraged to reflect together on the material from Phase 1. The theme of the Week of Prayer for Christian Unity in January 1987 also concerned the nature and purpose of the church.

Spring/autumn 1987 saw the third phase, which consisted of evaluation and proposals for action. At this point, three meetings were convened in the three regions (England, Wales and Scotland) to evaluate the Process and formulate proposals for a way forward. These were followed in September 1987, by a central, broadly representative conference of 330 Christians representing thirty-six churches and associations of churches. Those who attended this highly successful conference, which took place at Swanwick in Derbyshire,[4] agree that it worked because of a number of important features:

– Priority in the programme was given to time for worship and prayer. The conference was built around four times of corporate worship.

– A strong feeling of unity permeated everything. A representative of the Church of Scotland commented, 'There was a real sense of unity, of *coming together in our Father's presence* that in turn informed the working sessions, group and plenary as well as the equally important opportunities for informal conversations in the garden, at meals, and in the bar.'

– Discussion was grounded on the Bible. A leader of a black-led church wrote, 'I have been deeply

113

impressed by the emphasis of the Scriptures in this conference as compared to those in the conferences that I attended previously, especially from Roman Catholic Christians.'

– Some emphasis was placed upon repentance for past disunity, and there was a helpful session, led by Bishop Graham Chadwick, of prayer for 'healing of memories' related to personal hurt arising from disunity.

– Each church showed great concern for evangelism.

– Cardinal Hume, Archbishop of Westminster, made a vital contribution on behalf of the Roman Catholic Church by stating that he hoped that RC delegates would 'recommend to members of our church that we move now quite deliberately from a situation of co-operation to one of commitment to each other. By commitment to each other I mean that we commit ourselves to praying and working together for church unity, and to acting together, both nationally and locally, for evangelisation and mission.' The Roman Catholic church, which until that time had not been a member of the BCC thus declared itself (through the mouth of its leader in England and Wales) to be fully committed to the Inter-Church Process. This represented an exciting new development.

– The participation of black-led churches, including associations of churches such as the Afro-West Indian United Council of Churches and the West Indian Evangelical Alliance, was also a significant new departure.

The conference produced a 'Declaration' that was adopted and personally signed by all those present at Swanwick. They asked that it be read in churches on one of the Sundays in October 1987. In it, they declare, 'We now declare together our readiness to commit ourselves to each other under God. Our earnest desire is to become more fully, in His own time, the one Church of Christ, united in faith, communion, pastoral care and mission. . . . In the unity we seek we recognise that there will not be uniformity but legitimate diversity. . . . It is our conviction that, as a matter of policy at all levels and in all places, our churches must now move from co-operation to clear commitment to each other, in search of the unity for which Christ prayed, and in common evangelism and service of the world.'

In other words, ecumenism is no longer to be an extra activity for enthusiasts, but rather a dimension of all that we do, which releases gifts, ministries and resources. It means that churches should act with self-discipline to try, if possible, to work together rather than separately.

Practical proposals to come out of the conference included the setting up of regional councils for England, Wales and Scotland, and a combined council of churches for the UK and the Irish Republic.[5] These would all come into being in September 1990, and would replace the BCC (there is at present no Irish Council of Churches, although much dialogue and co-operation does take place). One can only admire the staff of the BCC for their personal commitment to the process, since all their contracts cease after 31st August, 1990.

Once the governing bodies of the various churches involved have responded to these proposals, the final year of the Process will be devoted to setting up the new bodies.

What does all this mean in terms of Christian unity in the terms that I have outlined in the previous chapters? I see in the whole Process various positive features. There is, first, a clear desire for *unity among leaders*. If there is to be unity of heart and mind between Christians, it is surely important that Christian *leaders* should be experiencing it. The meeting at Swanwick was itself partly a response to a grass-roots move towards unity at the local level. The leaders considered the question about the nature and purpose of the church in a prayerful, worshipful and biblical way. Comments of participants clearly indicate a sense that God was present in, and leading, the consultation. There was also a sense of deep fellowship.

115

The participants had a foretaste at Swanwick of the unity which they were seeking between the churches they represented. A youth delegate commented. 'In the quiet of God's House – TOGETHER, in prayer, in silence, in song, TOGETHER, in love with our living God we became a family. We were one.' Having experienced this, the leaders are now in a position to give a lead to their churches and denominations.

Then, there was the *wide spectrum of participating churches* at Swanwick. The Process of which the conference was a part had encouraged each denomination or grouping to reflect on and give an account of its own understanding of the Church. This had led to an interchange of insights. Christians were encouraged to listen humbly to one another at a national level in a way they probably had never done before.

The emphasis on the importance of *unity in diversity* in the Declaration rightly put paid to the model of unity which implies, 'To be fully united, everyone has to become like us'. Uniformity, under whatever denominational umbrella, is clearly not the goal of this particular Process. There was, too, a clear perception of unity as involving *whole churches* in sharing together in the tasks of evangelism, social action, prayer, etc., rather than as an ecumenical exercise participated in by at most 5 per cent of church members.

On the other hand, two questions remain. The first concerns *non-participating churches*. Clearly, each denomination has the responsibility of deciding for itself whether or not it participates in this particular Process at a national level. The most glaringly obvious absentees are the white-led Pentecostal denominations, Assemblies of God and Elim in particular. Also notable by their absence are those churches represented by the FIEC (Fellowship of Independent Evangelical Churches), and the House Churches. The Pentecostals, with well-established denominational structures, should surely consider carefully the wisdom of boycotting a new initiative which would benefit greatly from their involvement. The problem for the FIEC and House Churches is to decide how they should be represented – assuming that they want to be. The problem can't be insuperable, as other independent churches, e.g. the Brethren (whose watchword is the autonomy of the local congregation) and the Union of Welsh Independents, are both participating. On the other hand, the participating churches need to feel painfully the absence of these brothers and sisters in Christ. They have to ask themselves whether they have extended hands of love and fellowship with sufficient warmth and understanding. I personally look forward to the day when any inter-church structure set up nationally, at an intermediate (county or city) level, or at grass roots, will be able to incorporate these and other churches.

Second, and even more important, there are the *basic theological divisions* between the participating churches. In all the goodwill generated by a Process such as this, there is a tendency to overlook the doctrines that separate us. It is important that differences are not blurred. There is a great deal of painstaking work to be done, around the Scriptures, in the light of the Holy Spirit, paying due heed to the traditional interpretations of each church. Perhaps the most important question the churches need to agree on is, 'What is a Christian?' We must not dodge the issues.

There is another body in Britain that unites Christians and churches from a wide variety of denominational backgrounds: the *Evangelical Alliance (EA)*. It is probably not generally known that the EA has existed in this nation for over 120 years – far longer than the BCC. It has always sought to be a unifying force within British evangelicalism. In a recent book, Clive Calver, the present General Secretary of EA, gives a helpful overview of the developments in evangelicalism in the postwar years.[6] It is clear that the vast majority of evangelicals want to associate themselves, either as churches or as individuals, with the EA. Thus in the last decade, the EA had undergone a period of considerable growth which is not yet over. It now claims a membership of one million evangelicals, an estimate

117

taking into consideration both church and individual membership. Obviously, such a number of committed evangelicals speaking with a united voice have the potential to influence the government and society of Britain profoundly – which is what the EA leadership wants.

The EA differs from the BCC in being frankly confessional. To become a member, individuals or churches have to subscribe to a statement of faith which is detailed and uncompromising on issues such as substitutionary atonement and the physical return of Christ. As a result, the EA has built into it a powerful doctrinal basis for unity. Nevertheless, it would easily be possible for EA to split into a number of different constituencies. Calver identifies 'twelve tribes of evangelicalism', most of which are well represented in EA. These include such disparate elements as Anglican evangelicals, 'classical' Pentecostals, and House Churches. Probably the biggest and potentially the most damaging divide is between charismatics and non-charismatics. It is to the great credit of Clive Calver and his team that friendly and fraternal relationships have been maintained between these two camps – at least, within the membership of the EA.

In recent years, the EA has developed a wide range of concerns, resulting in various ministries presided over by a full-time staff of thirty. A recent issue of *Idea*, the EA quarterly bulletin, includes features on a Christian drug rehabilitation unit, a conference on 'Reaching the Nation's children', the problem of debt and how to solve it, and a major initiative for tackling the problems of unemployment in the inner cities – projects all sponsored either directly by the EA or by bodies that are members of it. Evangelicals can no longer be accused of an other-worldly approach to the problems of society. In particular, Evangelical Enterprise, launched in April 1987, has started significant unemployment projects throughout Britain on housing estates and in inner-city areas. These include a scheme in Chapletown, Leeds, in which fourteen churches have come together to form an inter-denominational employment project to refurbish a large building to house a community business consultancy.

The public face of the EA is most effectively shown at Spring Harvest, the inter-church festival and teaching conference which takes place for a three/four-week period at Easter. The EA does not directly organise Spring Harvest, but is closely associated with it. Spring Harvest started modestly in 1978 with 2,700 participants; ten years later, the numbers had grown to 58,000 (which, apparently, is a bigger gathering of Christians than any in the USA).

I have never been to Spring Harvest as a participant, but I did play it a flying visit last year in an attempt to interview Clive Calver. In the event, I arrived late for my appointment, and found him with only a few minutes to spare before a series of other meetings (that simply illustrates the pace of life for the organisers). The short time I spent in the holiday centre in Minehead, one of the venues where Spring Harvest takes place, convinced me that this was indeed a phenomenon of considerable significance. Clive invited me to go with him to a meeting of the staff: those working with children, teenagers, the counsellors, stewards, and so on. Immediate needs were shared, and we split up into small groups for prayer. Every detail of the conference was brought before God: young people on the verge of conversion, practical matters of organisation, leaders who were unwell. The concern to bathe everything in prayer was impressive, and it was clear that significant changes were taking place in people's lives as a result of the week's happenings (which included evangelistic meetings, with prayer for healing and deliverance, as well as teaching seminars, pop concerts and other special events of all sorts).

Afterwards, a small group of leaders gathered to talk informally. I was surprised by the number of nationally known people gathered together in one place at the same time, drawn from almost every denomination and shade of evangelical opinion. When Clive had found a little

119

more time to talk, I asked him how he thought the split between charismatic and non-charismatic evangelicals could be healed. He replied that this particular divide wasn't noticeable at Spring Harvest. There was unity in prayer, worship, evangelism and caring concern for the needy. The panel of preachers and teachers certainly contained people drawn from both camps. It seemed to me as though differences were being broken down in a very healthy way.

Later, strolling through a hall jam-packed with the stalls of every conceivable evangelical para-church organisation, I was hailed by someone I had last met in Nepal working for Operation Mobilisation. Here he was now, manning the OM stall. A few stalls further on, I chatted with the wife of the vicar I had worked with on 'Come Together' in Cambridge fifteen years before. Outside, I recognised the Rev Tony Higton and his wife, and was able to assure him of my support and prayers for his initiative to try to prevent the ordination of practising homosexuals to the ministry of the Church of England.

I mention these brief personal encounters simply as an illustration of the fact that there is an evangelical family within the Church in England that effectively cuts across the denominational boundaries. That family is growing daily and becoming more unified. In Clive Calver and his EA team it has an extremely able and articulate body of spokesmen. Though it represents only perhaps 16 per cent of the total church-going public, it can speak with a remarkably united and powerful voice. In a perceptive article in the *Independent* newspaper, Martin Wroe writes, 'The message is clear: Britain's evangelicals are on the move, adamant that they will no longer be confined to their narrow church-going ghettos, but will offer their spiritual medicine to a "morally sick" nation.'[7] It is clear that the EA *does* have a moral edge, with its support of the move to defeat the Government's Sunday Trading Bill, and its backing of the Alton Bill on abortion. Essentially, however, it does not seem to be so much a 'moral majority' as a spiritual movement aimed at preaching the Gospel effectively throughout the nation. Wroe quotes Roger Forster as saying (of the great 1988 'Make Way' march through London), 'It's a proclamation, a heavenly and earthly witness to the Lordship of Christ, shifting the spiritual state of the country.' This surely is at the heart of what the EA is all about.

After the BCC and EA, the most powerful unifying forces within the British churches are the *Special-Interest Groupings*. There have been at least two major national issues that have served as catalysts for Christian unity over the past few years. The first of these was the *Government's Bill to deregulate Sunday Trading*. Evangelicals were prominent in opposing this, notably through the Pro-Sunday Coalition, a ginger-group of six different organisations. The Bill was defeated, against all expectations, at its Second Reading in the Commons on 14th April, 1986, by just fourteen votes, despite the Government's majority of 138 and a three-line whip.

In a report issued by the Jubilee Centre (a Christian research centre into the nation's economic, political and social life, and a member of the coalition), the eight key factors which led to the defeat of the Bill are summarised. These include, among other things, research, a clear moral case, the involvement of many groups, and prayer. The groups concerned in fact included all the major church denominations. Particularly significant was a meeting four days before the parliamentary debate between the Home Secretary on the one hand, and the Archbishops of Canterbury (Anglican) and Westminster (R.C.) together with the Moderator of the Free Church Council on the other. The three church leaders expressed their united opposition to the Bill, and called for a free vote on the issue. The report comments, 'This was perhaps the first time since the Reformation that church leaders from all the three major segments of the church in Britain had together seen a senior Government minister.' In the course of the campaign, many thousands of letters were written by a wide variety of Christians to their MPs. Probably, many of these people had never done such a thing before. This enormous reaction spanned all denominational and even theological divides, uniting Protestants (both evangelical and liberal) and Roman Catholics.

Prayer about the issue was encouraged by the distribution of prayer cards, and many churches became involved in sustained prayer. On the day before the vote (which happened to be a Sunday), thousands of churches were praying that the Bill would be defeated. Its defeat the next day showed clearly what can be achieved by Christians powerfully united in prayer and political action under the guidance of the Holy Spirit.

The second political battle which united many Christians, but did not this time result in victory for them, was *the Liberal (now S.L.D.) MP David Alton's attempt to introduce a Private Member's Bill amending the time limit for abortions from twenty-eight to eighteen weeks.* The Bill was defeated on 6th May, 1988, when it was 'talked out' at its report stage. However, in the lengthy process leading up to the House of Commons debate, the issue had effectively united a vast number of Christians, both Roman Catholic and Protestant. The campaign was spearheaded by LIFE and SPUC (Society for the Protection of Unborn Children), both largely Roman Catholic, and CARE Campaigns, an evangelical Protestant organisation. Together with Alton, they presented a petition to the Prime Minister containing more than one million signatures. National prayer rallies on the issue such as Care for Life, in Royal Albert Hall, London (9th January, 1988) brought together members of all the major denominations. As a sign of unity, CARE, which organised the London rally, invited Cardinal Hume to lead the opening prayers. In an article in the evangelical monthly *Leadership Today*, Colin Blakely sums up Alton's achievement in these words: 'He united Christians – both Catholic and Protestant – in a way that few church leaders could achieve. He brought the abortion issue to the top of the public agenda. And although the Bill in its present form is dead, the battle is not over.'[8]

It is clear that there exist structures in England which can facilitate Christian unity at a national level. The

Inter-Church Process of the British Council of Churches is full of potential for deeper understanding and co-operation provided that it is rooted in shared prayer, worship and, above all, biblical truth. The Evangelical Alliance is providing an invaluable forum for once the deeply divided 'tribes of evangelicalism' to build bridges with one another and get a common vision. It seems to me important that these two bodies keep in close contact with each other, and proceed on the basis of mutual respect rather than mutual suspicion (there is, in fact, an increasing amount of helpful contact).[9] In addition to these structures, national events of political and moral significance clearly possess great power to draw Christians together from every denomination and grouping to be a force to be reckoned with in the nation. Together, these factors point to the possibility of a move of the Holy Spirit in our nation greater than anything we have seen so far this century, which could unite the churches to proclaim the gospel in power.

The situation in the UK is obviously unique, but it could provide some helpful guidelines in the search for Christian unity that is going on in other countries. It is surely helpful that a national council of churches should, if possible, exist in each country, and that it should sponsor meetings for consultation and prayer in which Christians can sense a unity in the Spirit. It is important that such councils take time to rethink their priorities and plan their future development in the sort of radical way adopted by the BCC. It is vital that evangelicals of all denominations unite nationally in an organisation like the EA, and in great gatherings for prayer, worship and teaching like 'Spring Harvest'. In addition, Christians in different countries should be sensitive to important national moral and spiritual issues that could join them in intercession and peaceful political action.

Finally, though, I have to state my belief that the unity goes on at a local level is at least as significant, in the long run, as the functioning of national councils and pressure-groupings. It is the job of the national bodies to give a clear lead, but to be effective, that lead has to be followed by all the Christians in the nation. Meanwhile, wherever local, inter-church groups of believers are meeting to pray, study the Bible, worship, evangelise, or minister to the needy, the true process of unity is going on, and the kingdom of God is being established on earth.

Chapter 9

Divided We Fall

Before looking at more specific ways in which Christians in England can move towards a deeper unity, we need to pause and consider three particularly glaring divisions between various groupings within the church, and how to overcome them. First, there is the relationship between evangelicals and Roman Catholics; second, that between evangelicals and 'liberal' Protestants; and finally, the main cause of division within evangelicalism – the so-called 'charismatic divide'. Each of these topics deserves a whole chapter (if not a book!) to itself, but I am simply going to make a few comments based on my own reading and experience, from an evangelical/ charismatic standpoint, concentrating particularly on how to make progress towards real unity.

First, *evangelicals and Roman Catholics*. The difficulties posed by Roman Catholicism for evangelicals would include first the *outer trappings* of worship – the contrast between candles, incense, statues and mystery on the one hand with simplicity and directness on the other. In the past, evangelicals would have been very suspicious of anything that smacked of the worship of images, and the use of candles as symbols of prayer to the saints or for the departed would have caused offence. Many would still find these things a reason for division. Others, however, would see such customs as symbolical, traditional and not constituting sufficient grounds for major disagreement. Many recent Roman Catholic services that I have attended have been in unadorned buildings, e.g. the chapels of religious communities, which have seemed, if anything, rather less cluttered than the average Anglican parish church.

Much more fundamental are the *theological differences*. These would include the role of Mary in salvation, prayer to Mary and the saints, the authority of Scripture over against tradition, the role of the papacy, the Mass, the doctrine of justification by faith, and the doctrine and practice of confession. These are a mixed bag; it seems to me that none is absolutely fundamental to the basic foundations of Christianity except that of *justification by faith*. The basic insight of Luther which led to the Reformation was that a person receives salvation as a free gift from God when he or she trusts in Christ, and not as a result of or reward for good deeds. In his book on Catholic/Protestant relations, *The Meeting of the Waters*, Bishop George Carey argues (with copious quotations) that most modern Roman Catholic theologians now accept that Luther was right.[1] If this is really so, Roman Catholics and evangelicals can unite on a bedrock of biblical truth. We clearly already agree on other fundamentals such as the divinity of Christ, his incarnation, atoning death, bodily resurrection, and second coming.

Evangelicals become worried when one of the more peripheral doctrines mentioned above threatens a clear biblical truth. So, for example, prayer to the saints or to Mary has no biblical basis, and also undermines the uniqueness of Jesus as the only one through whom we are to pray to the Father – or indeed as the Son of God to whom we are able to pray directly. My experience is that Catholics differ quite widely in the emphasis they put on the peripherals. Many, who are clearly born-again believers, are so Jesus-centred that they tend to ignore certain doctrines and practices. I well remember the American nun whom I met some years ago in Germany. She carried an enormous copy of the Bible (King James Version); the underlinings and notes on every page showed clearly that she knew it from cover to cover. We spent several days at an ecumenical centre together, and in the course of that time, she told me that she no longer felt able to pray the complete 'Hail Mary'. She could say the first half of the prayer (Gabriel's greeting to Mary) because it was biblical, but had felt compelled to change the second part, 'Holy Mary, mother of God, pray for us sinners now and at the hour of our death' by replacing 'Holy Mary, mother of God' with 'Blessed

Jesus, Son of God'. I am sure that, as God touches the hearts of many Catholics by his Spirit and teaches them through his word, many other similar adjustments are being made.

Evangelicals can view very positively the great changes that have taken place in the Roman Catholic church as a result of the Second Vatican Council (1962–5). Worship is now conducted mostly in the vernacular rather than in Latin, lay people have been encouraged to play a more important part in church life, and all Catholics have been urged to read and study the Bible for themselves. There has also been a significant change in the way Catholics think about unity. Protestant Christians are now referred to not as heretics but as 'separated brethren' whose Christian witness is to be treated with respect. Catholics now play as full a part as possible in local ecumenism, and, as we have seen, they are fully involved in the new 'Inter-Church Process' initiated by the BCC.

Another major influence that has drawn Catholics closer to some evangelicals is the charismatic movement within the R.C. church, often referred to as *Catholic Renewal*. This started in the USA in 1967, and has spread around the world. Charismatic evangelicals have been profoundly influenced by the unity they have sensed with charismatic Catholics whom they have met at conferences and in joint ministry. Typical of these would be the Anglicans Michael Harper and David Watson. The latter wrote in his autobiography, 'As I continued to ask the Spirit of God to change my negative attitudes I found that God was giving me an altogether new love towards many non-evangelicals, even Roman Catholics.'[2] Significantly, it is often Anglican charismatic evangelicals who find it most easy to feel at one with renewed Catholics. Anglicans are used to existing in a denomination that includes apparently opposite extremes. In the Anglican church, evangelicals know that they often have more in common with Anglo-Catholics than with middle-of-the-road liberals. Anglican evangelicals sense this same basic doctrinal unity with Roman Catholics. At least there isn't the

127

quibbling about the Incarnation, the Resurrection or the Atonement that one finds in liberal circles. Add the charismatic dimension, and you have a very strong sense of unity in the Spirit.

It is non-charismatic Free Church evangelicals who have the most difficulties uniting with Roman Catholics. There is a strong and understandable historical legacy of mistrust between such evangelicals and Catholics. The former can often only see the negatives: the unbiblical doctrines, and the fact that the Second Vatican Council, didn't go nearly far enough in reforming the church. They are, in any case, also deeply mistrustful of charismatic renewal, and its presence in the RC church only makes it more suspect! So the issue of Roman Catholicism only serves to fuel the division within English evangelicalism. The feelings of many free churchmen are summed up by Robert Amess, a Baptist, in his generally conciliatory book *One in the Truth?*: 'There seems among some Anglican Evangelicals not only a lack of interest in their Free Church brethren, but a positive seeking after unity with the Roman Catholic church that can only bring genuine disquiet to many'.[3]

I confess unashamedly that my own position is that of Harper and Watson – predictably, perhaps, because of my Anglican background. Nevertheless, I feel that my reasons are sound. If an individual Roman Catholic is truly born again, then there is no reason on earth why I or any other believer should not enjoy full fellowship with him, within the constraints of church discipline. 'How do you know that he is born again?', you may object. But the same question might be asked about any Protestant. My answer would be that you must give any professing Christian the benefit of the doubt, until you get to know them better and can begin to sense whether they really are a Christian from their quality of life – the 'fruit' which, Jesus teaches, is the best test of a true believer (Matt.7.16).

In order to improve relations between evangelicals and Roman Catholics, it is vitally important, first, that they get to know each other. We need to seize every opportunity for friendship and dialogue. This is not easy, as we move in very different constituencies. All the more reason why we should make the effort! This in fact happened on a large scale in house groups organised specially for the BCC Lent course in 1987. It is easiest for charismatics in both camps to do this, as they have a very great deal in common in terms of experience of the powerful working of the Holy Spirit.

Then, as we begin to know each other, we sense the Lord's presence in one another (if we truly are Christian), and are able to share in prayer and worship together. I have done this in very large gatherings, and one-to-one meetings, but have yet to experience joint prayer in a small group made up of both Protestants and Catholics. One day I shall, and I am looking forward to it.

We can certainly share in 'Jesus action', ministry to the poor and needy. In fact, the RC church has a lot to teach evangelicals in this sphere. There has never been a lack of Catholics who are willing to give unstintingly of themselves to help the poor. The most obvious and much-admired example of this is Mother Theresa of Calcutta, but there are countless others who take this particular path of discipleship. We can also, I believe, evangelise jointly, preferably on the basis of a brief shared, biblically-grounded statement of faith, though this is not essential. I have been impressed with RC participation in 'Mission England' and 'Make Way' marches.

Roman Catholics and evangelicals also often unite on moral issues that affect society. Two obvious recent examples have been their support for the Alton Bill to limit abortions, and their identical objections to the film, *The Last Temptation of Christ*, which gives a highly distorted picture of Jesus. Evangelicals of all persuasions recognise that Roman Catholics have a proper and biblical concern for the sanctity of life and the divinity of Christ. Equally, we should be prepared to recognise that they may very well be just as much born-again believers as we are, and act accordingly.

The dialogue between *evangelicals* and *liberals* is a more difficult one to pursue. I have already defined the word 'liberal' in its theological sense in Chapter 1. I can speak with a certain amount of authority, as I was once a liberal myself – not a very way-out one, it is true, but certainly influenced in that direction by my theological training. I have also sometimes experienced acute tension in my relationships with liberal colleagues ever since I myself became an evangelical. My conclusion is that the relationship between evangelicals and liberals is likely to be very difficult indeed. This is because there are major points of theological disagreement, and positions tend to be held with quite a lot of ill-feeling. At worst, evangelicals consider liberals to be heretically unbiblical, while liberals see evangelicals as narrow-minded, unthinking and obscurantist.

Difficulties in finding common ground appear to be legion. The most basic division is over attitudes to the Bible. Evangelicals assert (in the words of the EA Basis of Faith) 'the divine inspiration of Holy Scripture and its consequent entire trustworthiness and supreme authority in all matters of faith and conduct.' Liberals tend to see it as an historical collection of books which point to truths about God and man, but which Christians may interpret in very varied ways to suit their own understanding of life and faith.

Obviously, evangelicals vary widely in their interpretation of certain biblical passages, but they never doubt that they are inspired by the Holy Spirit. Liberals, on the other hand, can happily discount whole tracts of the Bible. An elderly former colleague of mine, for example, used to maintain indignantly that Jesus could not possibly have uttered the words recorded in Matthew chapter 23, where he criticises the Pharisees in very outspoken terms, calling them, among other things, 'hypocrites', 'sons of hell', 'whitewashed tombs', and 'brood of vipers'. According to my friend, Jesus was much too nice and loving to have said such things. Also, he felt, the Pharisees were too holy and righteous to have had such things said about them by Jesus. In other word, Matthew chapter 23 was an invention of the writer's, probably reflecting the anti-Pharisee feeling of the early church at a time of persecution. The fact that Jesus might actually have spoken the words substantially as recorded, and that his assessment of the Pharisees might have been correct, never entered my friend's head. In other words, he was looking in the Bible for a Jesus of the sort that he wanted to find. Any characteristics or words which did not agree with his particular Jesus were rejected out of hand.

That sort of view of the Scriptures can be described as 'old-fashioned' nineteenth-century liberalism in that it at least attempts to find a historical Jesus behind the biblical account. A more recent, and more potent form of biblical liberalism is represented by the theology of the German New Testament scholar Rudolf Bultmann. Bultmann felt that the New Testament was so overlaid with 'mythological' trappings (e.g. angels, demons, miracles) that in order to make it intelligible to modern man, with his scientific understanding, it had to be radically 'demythologised'. As a result, he re-interpreted anything that was supernatural, totally rejecting the fact that it might actually have happened as recorded. He also used existentialist philosophy to interpret the New Testament, which led him to devalue its importance as a historical record, and over-emphasise its significance for believers now.

These two aspects of his methodology led him into serious theological difficulties with both the Incarnation and the Resurrection. As the New Testament portrays these events as both supernatural and historical, Bultmann had to re-interpret them in a very radical way. So, for example, according to him the Resurrection is only important in so far as it resulted in the Easter faith of the disciples. He wrote, of the disciples' decision to follow Jesus after the Crucifixion and Resurrection, 'How this act of decision took place in detail, how the Easter faith arose in individual disciples, has been obscured in the

tradition by legend and is not of basic importance. . . .
The accounts of the empty grave, of which Paul still
knows nothing, are legends'.[4]

There is much more that could be said about the
theology of Bultmann; the short extracts above merely
give a taste of his views. His works are brilliant,
scholarly, and intended for academics only. The fact
is, however, that his ideas have permeated deep into
the consciousness of most contemporary New Testament
scholars, who have then taught them, usually in a
watered-down form, to at least two generations of
students like myself. The non-evangelical Protestant
pastors and ministers of the Western world (and,
increasingly, of the rest of the world), have been fed
on a diet of predigested Bultmann and his pupils, as I was
at both Edinburgh and Harvard universities. The result
is that the Bible becomes shifting sand, a mysteriously
complicated book which cannot be trusted to say what
really happened. To take it at face value is derided as
'naïve', 'fundamentalist', or 'simplistic'.

There are, however, a good number of excellent
biblical scholars who do not take the Bultmannian line.
Many of these are evangelicals, such as F. F. Bruce,
Donald Guthrie and I. H. Marshall, and the quality of
their work is so outstanding that they cannot possibly
be ignored. The pity is that such scholars are very
seldom recommended on university theological reading
lists. Certainly, I was never made aware of them. At
evangelical colleges, however, students are naturally
encouraged to read commentaries and scholarly works
that uphold the historicity and inspiration of Scripture,
at the same time as confronting the problems that
undoubtedly exist in the text.

Largely as a result of the influence of Bultmann, who
was himself influenced by a century of sceptical German
biblical scholarship, liberals have tended to doubt some
of the fundamental doctrines of Christianity. The Virgin
Birth has for a long time been a prime target (the
young William Temple, later to become Archbishop of
Canterbury, and hardly a radical by today's standards,

was for a while refused ordination because he had problems in believing in it). This has led to some radical re-interpretations of the Incarnation (e.g, in *The Myth of God Incarnate,* a collection of essays by some British theologians).[5] Liberals have always disliked the doctrine of substitutionary atonement, although it is clearly biblical, because to them it portrays God as an angry sadist. They fail to see that Jesus was a willing victim, fully co-operating with the Father in his work of redemption. Probably the liberal difficulty in seeing Jesus as fully God makes it difficult for them to accept the doctrine. If Jesus is just the best man who ever lived, the substitutionary atonement does indeed become meaningless, or horrific, because it does imply that God is a vengeful monster. The bodily resurrection has recently been in the news because of its radical re-interpretation by David Jenkins, Bishop of Durham – clearly, he is deeply influenced by Bultmann. Also in doubt is the bodily ascension of Jesus. The fact that he ascended in his transformed resurrection body doesn't solve the problem for the liberals, because they question Jesus' bodily resurrection anyway.

And so one could go on. As a result of their radically different approaches to Scripture, liberals and evangelicals divide on almost every basic Christian doctrine. To a liberal, miracles are by definition impossible because 'science' has disproved them (though this is, in fact, a very unscientific approach!). The Holy Spirit is simply 'God in everyone', 'the Ground of our being', and prayer is quietly being in touch with him. Personal ethics become a matter of doing what seems to you to be the most loving thing in the circumstances, not of observing the teaching of the Bible with the help of the Holy Spirit. Salvation becomes universal, because a loving liberal God could not possibly allow anyone, even Hitler, to go to hell or even be snuffed out for ever. Other religions are not human and sinful ways of trying to reach God, but valid paths to God on a par with the biblical revelation. Finally, the Second Coming has either already happened in the First Coming ('realised eschatology'), or is simply a symbol for the perfect future towards which mankind is striving. It is not surprising that to evangelicals, liberals seem to be preaching another gospel altogether.

In the light of what I have written, it might seem that there is no possibility for unity between evangelicals and liberals. However, hope lies, first, in the fact that not all liberals are anything like as extreme as I have portrayed them. I can testify from personal experience that many liberal ministers are sincere and committed Christians who have become confused in their theology because of what they have been taught at college or university. I certainly came into that category myself. Some of the more radical liberal scholars were even leading lights of their university Christian Unions in their student days! For them, the move to a liberal view of the Bible has probably seemed a part of their maturing as people from being crassly narrow-minded to being more open to other ideas.

I have found that many (though not all) of my liberal friends are quite open to more conservative theological positions, particularly charismatic teaching on the doctrine of the Holy Spirit, the experience of his power, and the exercise of his gifts. When the young Pentecostal minister David du Plessis was told by God through a prophecy to visit the headquarters of the World Council of Churches, he found that the liberals there gave him a very warm welcome.[6] The danger is that such warmth turns out to be simply superficial friendliness, coupled with an interest in religious phenomena, while real theological differences are glossed over. But I believe that evangelicals should take every opportunity of meeting with liberal Christians, engaging in dialogue with them, and courteously putting forward a truly biblical form of Christianity. For example, I have frequently been asked by liberals to speak on charismatic renewal at ministers' fraternals, clergy training days, home groups and so on. My words have always met with a mixed reception, and I have frequently felt like Daniel in the lions' den. But I have always found that the opportunity was worthwhile and valuable as a bridge-building exercise. The recent joint volume by the liberal David Edwards and the evangelical John Stott is a model of gracious and scholarly debate.[7]

It is of basic importance for evangelicals and liberals to get to know one another. This can be done at leadership level through local ministers' fraternals, and at grass-roots level through Lent groups and any other contact that the local council of churches can organise. Evangelicals must realise that Christians who hold a liberal position may have what to them is a valid reason for rejecting some part of the Bible. For example, they may feel that God as portrayed in the Old Testament is vengeful and inferior in moral quality to God in the New Testament. This view is understandable, particularly if Christians have never received any clear explanation which is based on the essential unity and truthfulness of the Scriptures. It is also good that the Inter-Church Process contains both evangelicals and liberals, because this means that dialogue is going on at a national level.

There seems to me to be no reason why liberals and evangelicals should not pray and worship together provided that it is clear that they are all worshipping the God and Father of our Lord Jesus Christ. They can also collaborate most helpfully in community action such as street-warden schemes, caring for the elderly and housebound, and looking after the homeless. Liberals are at their strongest in the area of social justice, and evangelicals increasingly share their biblical concern for righteousness in Britain and overseas.

Joint evangelism is more tricky. It seems that, as with Roman Catholics, this is most easily done on the basis of a brief shared statement of faith. I am personally looking forward to seeing more and more liberals realising the value and truth of the Scriptures coupled with the supernatural power of God. As they see society crumbling around them they will recognise that biblical Christianity in action is the only authentic life-changing answer to people's needs.

Finally, what is to be done about the *charismatic divide* between evangelicals? There have been a number of voices raised in recent years lamenting evangelical disunity. These critics have lamented a lack, not of doctrinal unity, but of *love*. The sociologist and prophet Clifford Hill, who himself moved, as I did, from a liberal position to an evangelical one, wrote in 1980, 'I was really looking forward to working among the Bible-believing Christians as I thought that the tensions of working with people of widely different beliefs would disappear and there would be unity of purpose and love for one another. I thought I would be leaving behind the old jealousies and feuds that are part of the liberal scene and I would find harmony among those who all accept the authority of Scripture. Incredibly I have found greater disunity in the evangelical world than anything I had previously known. Moreover, I've found less love!'[8]

The radio journalist Nick Page makes the same point in a leading article in *Leadership Today*: 'Why do we evangelicals, while rightly upholding the authority of Scripture so often neglect its strong teaching on love? Can't we disagree and do so forthrightly, without imputing wrong motives to each other and without declaring our brother's language, church, attitude during worship, etc., etc., beyond the pale or unbiblical?'[9] Finally, in a deeply felt plea for unity from within the 'reformed' constituency of evangelicalism, Robert Amess declares, 'Evangelicalism today is not marked by mutual trust and affection but rather distrust, recrimination and animosity. . . . There is a love of controversy within Evangelicalism today, a contentious spirit, a party mentality that has never been so prevalent before.'[10] If this criticism is justified (and I believe that it is), how is it that Christians who believe that the Bible is the inspired word of God so flout it?

There are a number of issues which clearly divide evangelicals. These include theological differences, e.g. between Calvinists and Arminians, those who hold opposing views on the Second Coming, and those who disagree over infant baptism; differences in people's understanding of the church, represented mainly by the split between the House Churches and the historic denominations; and socio-cultural differences, seen for example in the existence of white-led and black-led churches.[11] But I would see the chief problem now centring around the split between charismatic and non-charismatic evangelicals.

When the Pentecostal movement first began in 1900, it caused very negative reactions in most other evangelicals. They felt that the supernatural gifts of the Spirit were given to enable the first-century church to become firmly established, and that they were withdrawn after the generation of the original apostles. In support of this they cited I Corinthians, chapter 13, verses 9 to 12, which very few scholars nowadays would seriously accept as relevant. They also questioned the theology of a 'second blessing' after conversion, particularly when it was held that this 'baptism in the Holy Spirit' had to be authenticated by speaking in tongues, maintaining that such a position could not be held absolutely from Scripture. As a result, Pentecostalism remained quite distinct and isolated from the rest of 'mainstream' evangelicalism. However, as soon as Pentecostal theology and experience began to affect the historic denominations through the charismatic movement of the 1950s and 1960s, evangelicals within those churches were the people most profoundly affected. This led to a further split within evangelicalism which is still adversely affecting relationships.

The danger for the charismatics was that they would see themselves as a spiritual élite, super-Christians who could look down patronisingly on their less dynamic brethren who had not been 'baptised in the Spirit'. Most uncritically adopted a two-stage view of Christian initiation (conversion followed by 'baptism in the Spirit') without sufficient scriptural backing. The danger for the non-charismatics was that they would retrench in their existing positions and miss out on what was a genuine move of the Holy Spirit within the churches. They were so suspicious of anything even faintly emotional that such phenomena as speaking in tongues, weeping, laughing or shaking filled them with alarm. Some were also prevented by their traditional interpretation of Scripture from accepting that God could or would perform miraculous signs and wonders nowadays. Prophecy, too, was highly suspect because it seemed to undermine the vital importance of the Bible in guiding and teaching the flock. This difference of opinion soon hardened into a split, which was then fostered with acrimony and suspicion. Even in the late 1970s, after a lot of public debate on the subject in print, I remember a Bristol University student politely handing me back books by David Watson and Michael Harper that I had lent him, on the grounds that his pastor did not approve of the authors' views, and had advised him not to read them as they would be unhelpful.

Since the arrival on our shores of the so-called 'Third Wave' of Renewal through the ministry of John Wimber, on yearly visits since 1984, the debate has gone on with even greater intensity.[12] It now centres very much around miraculous signs and wonders: whether they are authentic, and whether they are an essential part of the Gospel for the Western world in our generation. Many non-charismatics are changing their views, which must be very threatening to those who are 'holding the line'.

There have, however, from the early 1970s, been a number of positive moves to heal the rift. Within the Anglican evangelical constituency, for example, a group of leaders representing both points of view met and produced a joint statement entitled *Gospel and Spirit*. They reached agreement that experiences of the grace of God which have 'deep and transforming significance' can happen subsequent to conversion, though they disagreed about the correct way of describing them. They add, 'We urge one another and all our fellow-Christians to press on to know the Lord better, and thus to enter into the fulness of our inheritance in Christ.' On the gifts of the Spirit, they clearly affirm that they 'see no reason why such gifts should not be given and exercised today.'[13] Other writers similarly rejected the two-stage theory, but warmly endorsed the teaching that spiritual gifts are for every age, including our own.

So, for example, co-authors Donald Bridge and David Phypers (Baptist and Anglican respectively) wrote, 'It seems, then, that the idea of gifts being withdrawn from the church at the end of the first century is not in itself capable of scriptural proof.' They go on to assert, speaking of our own generation, 'Indeed, as the century draws towards its close, the church would seem to need the benefits of spiritual gifts more than ever before.'[14]

An increasing number of evangelicals have come to endorse this point of view. They would teach that part of being a Christian is to enter into a daily experience of the power and love of the Spirit, and that supernatural spiritual gifts are available now to be received from God and used in his service. An initial experience of the spirit in this way could be called 'baptism in the spirit' (though they would avoid that term), but it would in fact simply be the first conscious manifestation of what is already our heritage in Christ. It might well be accompanied by speaking in tongues, but this is not a necessary sign of the Spirit's anointing. I suspect that theologically this explanation makes much more sense to the majority of British evangelicals than the traditional Pentecostal teaching, and it has won over many doubters. John Wimber strongly agrees, teaching that whereas Pentecostals are strong on experience but weak on theology, evangelicals are weak on experience but strong on theology. Many evangelicals have been deeply affected by his teaching, and are now developing new models of ministry and evangelism which include healing, deliverance, and all the spiritual gifts.

Nevertheless, problems remain. Every town or city in England has one or two leading evangelical churches, and several smaller ones, which will not tolerate any form of charismatic teaching – even the modified form outlined above. This may be for one of several reasons. Some, particularly ministers, have had really bad experiences with divisive and difficult charismatics in their church in the past, and are thus inclined to distrust anyone who wants to use spiritual gifts publicly. Others feel that they are temperamentally unsuited to a charismatic style of doing things, as they are too unemotional, intellectual or analytical. Still others probably find that the way they do things in their church suits them very well, and is having excellent results in terms of conversion-growth and lives transformed. They see no reason for change.

I do not find any of these reasons convincing, but they serve to preserve the status quo. Any minister who holds them will effectively act as a cork in the bottle, preventing any new charismatic development from taking place in his church. I have every sympathy with ministers of highly effective non-charismatic churches which God is using wonderfully, particularly in evangelism. In their position, I too might be loath to rock the boat by importing new ideas and practices, particularly if I were not theologically convinced by them. Experience has shown, however, that churches that do take the plunge in this way may lose some members (though with sensitive leadership, they will not), but eventually gain far more through the renewing and reviving work of the Spirit.

It is particularly heartening that more friendly relationships are being established across the charismatic divide. This is clearly demonstrated at Spring Harvest. As we have seen, the General Secretary of EA, Clive Calver, maintains that in that setting, the division simply does not exist.

The reason for this is partly, no doubt, sensitive worship-leading that steers a careful course between extremes, partly a sense of real Christian fellowship and unity on fundamentals which a residential convention encourages, but mainly the presence and power of the Holy Spirit. John Noble describes the final communion service of Spring Harvest in a recent book: 'The bread and wine came round. Who would have guessed we were from divided churches? Who would have thought we represented such different views and perspectives? Who would have thought that a few short years ago this would have been impossible? We embraced one another, eating and drinking together, singing to Jesus who had accomplished it, first quietly, the triumphantly.'[15]

I believe that it will be through shared evangelism that the two sides will unite most powerfully. It is fascinating to see missions like open Air Campaigners (OAC) which started as staunchly non-charismatic, realising that God heals people on the streets, and adjusting their methods accordingly. It is good to know of evangelists, like Eric Delve, increasingly prepared to pray for healing and deliverance at their meetings. I make no secret of being a fully paid-up charismatic; but I do fear for the future of renewal if the power of the Spirit is kept locked up as the special preserve of a holy huddle of churchy enthusiasts. You can't keep the Holy Spirit in a box, anyhow! He wants to be out on the streets, meeting needs and transforming lives as the Gospel of the Kingdom of Jesus Christ is proclaimed. John Wimber has taught us about the effectiveness of 'power evangelism', preaching accompanied by miracles, healings and deliverances. It is up to us to put this into practice, not simply to set up a healing group in our church. Conversely, non-charismatics need to realise that they need all the spiritual gifts if they are to be fully effective evangelists.

Evangelicals have an enormous responsibility in England. We have a right understanding of the Bible as the inspired Word of God. We believe in the supernatural power of the Holy Spirit, at any rate in theory. We should be the Christians who are unitedly spearheading the moving of God in our nation. Instead, we bicker and fight over inessentials, leaving the high ground to the Roman Catholics, with their disciplined and united stand for the basics of the faith and its moral implications, and the liberals, with their burning concern for social justice. The EA is doing a grand job in bringing us together, but it is up to us to get our inner attitudes right. We must not fail our generation. I believe that the answer lies in our discovering together a strong, vibrant faith, in which biblical truth is embodied in the power and love of the Holy Spirit, working through all the spiritual gifts to build up the church and to reach out into our desperately needy society both to save sinners and transform evil structures.

PART IV

Future Perfect?

Chapter 10

One Local Church

We have seen in Chapter 8 some of important moves towards unity that are going on at a national level. Far more significant for the future, however, are the local developments. It is in our city, town or neighbourhood that we have to work out the principles taught by national leaders. This is as it should be, if we remember that one of the definitions of 'church' is 'all the Christians in a particular city or locality'.[1]

It was vital to God's plan that the Holy Spirit fell upon the disciples in a particular place, *Jerusalem*. God did not cause the church to emerge spontaneously in fifty different villages in Israel. Jerusalem, the centre of Jewish life and worship, the place where Jesus died and rose again, was central to his purposes. The church had to start there.

As the book of Acts traces the development of church around the Eastern Mediterranean, it becomes apparent how important it is what route the Gospel takes, and *cities* assume great significance in God's plan of action. From Jerusalem, the spotlight moves on to *Samaria* in Acts chapter 8, where we see Philip, the evangelist, preaching the gospel with tremendous results. The fact that the word goes out first to the despised Samaritans shows graphically how in Christ God has broken down every man-made barrier that divides races and cultures. Then in chapter 11, we read how the church is established in *Antioch*. Antioch was a thriving city with a fine seaport. It was there that the first Gentile church was founded; we learn from Acts chapter 11, verses 21 and 26, that it was a large church. From there, Paul and Barnabas set out on their first missionary journey (Acts 13.3), and Antioch was to become a great 'sending church', which strongly favoured a ministry to both Jews and Gentiles. Its role in the planting of new churches in Asia Minor and Greece was crucial. Paul's second and third missionary journeys also started there.

As we read the account in Acts of Paul's journeys, we are again struck by the importance of cities and towns. Paul's clear strategy was to establish congregations of believers in every main centre of population to which God directed him. He did this by first preaching in the synagogue, where he was (initially at any rate) welcome as a rabbi, and then, after his message had, invariably, divided the congregation, and he had been shown the door, turning his attention to the Gentiles. A typical example of this procedure is the account of how the church was planted at *Pisidian Antioch* (Acts 13.13–52). Paul and his companions attend the synagogue on the Sabbath, and are actually invited to bring a 'message of encouragement' (v.15). What an evangelistic opportunity! Paul certainly makes the most of it, and he is given a good hearing. Many Jews are interested in what he has to say, and he is invited to speak again the following Sabbath (vv. 42–3). This time, however, he has a much more hostile reception (v.45). Paul and Barnabas therefore turn to the Gentiles, and make a number of converts (v.48). However, the hostile Jews stir up a persecution against Paul and his team, and they are forced to depart in a hurry (v.50), leaving behind a considerable number of believers, both Jews and Gentiles. Later, on their return journey, they revisit Pisidian Antioch, where they strengthen the church and appoint elders before sailing home (vv. 21–8).

We know too that Paul was prepared to spend considerable time establishing strong churches in cities that were clearly important in the ancient world. For example, he stayed at least eighteen months in *Corinth*, a large and wealthy city which controlled the trade routes across Greece. (Acts 18.11). Paul knew that a strong church planted there could influence visitors from all parts of the Empire. *Ephesus* was equally, if not more, important as the leading commercial, political and religious centre in the Roman province of Asia, and Paul stayed there for more than two years. During that time, he founded a church which was to become the foremost of the seven important churches in Asia Minor addressed in chapters 2 and 3 of Revelation. His final destination was *Rome* itself, the imperial capital. A church had already been established there before he arrived as a prisoner; in his letter to the Roman Christians, he addresses them as 'all in Rome who are loved by God and called to be saints' (Romans 1.7). Still, he realised the evangelistic potential of the great city, for he goes on to write, 'I planned many times to come to you . . . in order that I might have a harvest among you, just as I have had among the other Gentiles' (v.13).

To Paul the church-planter, any city presented a challenge for the gospel. It's not surprising, then, to find in his letters to various churches that his view of a church is defined first of all by *where it is*. He writes to the church in Rome, Corinth, Ephesus, Philippi, Colossi, Thessalonica, or to the churches of Galatia (an entire province). Each local church seems to be independent of the others in the conduct of its affairs. The local church would clearly value the ministry and respect the authority of genuine apostles, particularly those who founded it, though it is clear from the Corinthian letters that Paul had to cope in Corinth with false apostles who criticised his teaching and undermined his authority (II Cor. 11.1–15). Local churches did depend on one another for practical support: we know that from the collection organised by Paul for the Jerusalem church (II Cor. 8–9). The one local church which appears to have dominated the others was the Jerusalem church, because of the Jewish Christians there insisting on the circumcision of Gentile converts (see Gal. 2.11–4). At the Council of Jerusalem (Acts 15.1–31), this disagreement was resolved, and henceforth the local churches were able to develop freely without any heavy-handed interference from Jerusalem.

If the importance of the church in a locality is so clear in the New Testament, why have we so completely lost sight of it since? The first reason is *the development of church leadership structures*. Initially, the leadership of the Church became more dominated by individuals (bishops) rather than groups of elders with a presiding elder. The bishop's jurisdiction widened to include the whole region surrounding the city where his church was situated (the diocese). Then, dioceses were grouped together under senior leaders (archbishops or patriarchs) who exercised an authority that became increasingly dominant, and, eventually, as much political as spiritual.

The second reason now appears: *the rise of denominations.* When more than one 'stream' of Christianity had arisen side by side in the same city, with one group persecuting the other (e.g. Catholics versus Montanists), 'true' Christianity became defined by what structure you belonged to (with its particular theology and practices) rather than by the town in which you lived. This situation has been the norm in England since the Reformation, when dissenting groups were present (though illegal) from the start. Free Church worship has been legal since 1689, Roman Catholic worship only since 1791. With the explosion of new denominations in the twentieth century, the scene is now bewilderingly complex. A town of 100,000 inhabitants might have not only ten to twenty Anglican parishes, two or three Roman Catholic parishes, and a full range of Free Churches (including the two main Pentecostal denominations, several small Brethren assemblies, and a few Free Evangelical churches), but possibly two largish House Churches and some black-led churches as well.

It seems to me that if we are to reverse the trend of centuries, and pray and work for Christians to express real, visible unity, we need to follow the biblical pattern. As we have seen, the Bible defines 'church' in three ways as *universal, city-wide,* and *house-based.* Applying this threefold classification to our contemporary situation, we should therefore understand 'the church in the house' to be expressed both by house groups within a local church and by that local church itself, seen as a self-contained unit regardless of denomination. The 'city church' or 'church in the locality' would then be the sum total of all these local churches.

This sounds simple enough, but it's very difficult to put into practice. For a start, each denomination has built up a very strong structure of its own. In the Church of England, for example, we find three tiers: the parish, the deanery and the diocese, each with its council or synod. The clergy met regularly in 'chapters', which most of them would regard as more important than the local interdenominational 'ministers' fraternal'. There are other groupings of clergy along 'party' lines, notably the Diocesan Evangelical Fellowships and 'Eclectics' groups (for younger evangelical ministers). In other words, it's a full-time job being an Anglican, particularly if you're a clergyman. There are similar structures and demands in all denominations, without exception. Even a 'non-denominational', non-aligned church such as my own has meetings involving other similar churches. Christians, especially leaders, who also involve themselves in inter-denominational activities have to be extremely keen and well-motivated.

This introduces the third factor working against the 'city church' concept: *human weakness and sin.* We are either too tired, too preoccupied with 'doing our own thing' (especially if our church is thriving), too scared of the unknown, or too disdainful of associating with 'heretics', to put a very high priority on relating to the brothers and sisters who aren't members of our particular ecclesiastical club.

All this is surely sad and profoundly wrong. God wants us to express genuine unity. He wants us to love one another as he loves us. A wife and husband can't express love to one another telepathically, or if they are living completely separate lives. In fact, a sure sign that a marriage is in difficulties is when the partners aren't communicating verbally. Christians from different denominations and traditions need to take seriously the fact that we must communicate across the man-made denominational fences with their brothers and sisters on the other side. To do this, we have to take risks and be vulnerable.

Let me give a personal example. There was a time when I feared and despised evangelicals. They represented to me the worst sort of narrow puritanism and theological

149

obscurantism. Then one day I found that my world had been turned upside-down. I had rashly allowed the Holy Spirit to have free reign in my life, and he had set to work on my thought-processes. All sorts of questions were churning round in my mind. Could the Bible be taken much more literally than I had ever believed possible? Can God still break into space and time in supernatural and miraculous ways? By the grace of God, this was happening at Cambridge University, where there is no shortage of respected evangelical scholars of the sort that could help me. I remember going to one of them in a terrible state, full of fears about committing intellectual suicide. He was a research student, younger than I, and he might have reacted with alarm at having to cope with the Chaplain of King's in a flap. In fact, he couldn't have been kinder, more relaxed, or more reassuring. But funnily enough – and here I will doubtless shock some readers – the thing that impressed me more than anything about him was he offered me a glass of port! Here was no narrow puritan fanatic, but someone that I could relate to, given my particular background. Over the port we talked and prayed. And God gave me peace.

I have since come to love and accept evangelicals; in fact, I am happy to accept the label myself (I am a member of the EA). But the essential thing is not that each Christian should join the evangelical club, the charismatic club, or a society (such as Eclectics) within a particular denomination. It is rather that we should learn to accept each other as members of God's family, with all our differences, listen to one another, and treat each other with kindness and loyalty. We should not try to shape each other into our particular mould. That is a pressurising and ultimately fruitless exercises. Rather, we should each try to express our faith in a way that is as true, genuine and biblical as possible, and do as much as we can together to express our unity rather than our differences. This will take time and demand self-sacrifice, but that is part of the cost of discipleship. We are all so busy with the affairs of our little churches (and by world standards, even the largest local churches in

Britain are pretty small) that we don't give nearly a high enough priority to the wider vision of the church in the locality.

However, I believe that all over this country the tide is turning. There is a new awareness of the need for Christians to unite. The historic denominations are, on the whole, suffering from numerical decline in membership. Their members and leaders are only too aware of this. Their response is either to retrench and plan for decline, continuing with the mixture as before, or to take the much more perilous course of a radical change of direction. Unless they are totally blind to the realities of the situation, they must realise that there are by and large two sorts of church within their denomination which are thriving, not declining.

First, there are the *evangelical* churches, which believe what the Bible says about the necessity of mission and personal conversion, and are actively reaching out with the gospel into the non-Christian community; then, there are the *charismatic* ones, where there is a high expectation of the supernatural working of the Holy Spirit in healing, prophecy and other gifts. Churches that are both evangelical and charismatic are like dynamite, and there are more and more of them. In the Church of England for example, centres of renewal like Holy Trinity, Brompton, Emmanuel Church, Hawkwell, and St. Andrew's, Chorleywood are having a profound effect both in areas where they are and on the national church scene.

The only denominations to be seeing consistently high growth, which are mainly House Church and both black-led and mainstream Pentecostal, are becoming increasingly evangelistic and also gradually more open to contact with other local churches of different denominations. They have something important to give, and they want to share it. Unfortunately, some House Churches until comparatively recently adopted a position of superiority which implied, 'We're the best thing since sliced bread. If you want what we've got to offer, you need to join us'. But there seems to be a welcome change of attitude. Hands of friendship are now being reached out, not from a great height, but from a position of equality.

How, then, can Christians make the biblical pattern of the 'city church' a reality in the incredibly different situation today? I believe that the following practical steps are essential, assuming that we have the right humble, loyal and forgiving attitudes to the other local churches:

To start with, *we must stop thinking denominationally.* In fact, we'll probably have to develop two ways of thinking. The less important of the two will have to do with our denomination, its committees, services, societies, missions, stewardship campaigns, and so on. The more important will have to do with the entire body of truly committed Christians living in a city (or area within a city), town, or village, including the Christians who live in the area but go to a church outside it (these people are sometimes difficult to locate!).

This means, in practical terms, that *we must use every available existing structure to express our unity.* These include, first, *the local council of churches.* Sometimes we may find that some of the activities planned by the council are a waste of time, but at least, if we are members, we have a right to say so! I can understand a local church standing aloof from a council of churches because a lot of what is discussed seems, quite frankly, rather marginal. I've been chairman of a council of churches, and I know that there are a certain amount of routine events which mark the 'ecumenical year': Christian Aid Week, the Week of Prayer for Christian Unity, the churches' float for the local carnival, and so on. A keen evangelical church will not find this type of programme very relevant to the pressing task of preaching the gospel. It will prefer to support Tear Fund rather than Christian Aid, the EA Week of Prayer rather than Unity Week. I also respect (though I do not agree with) the attitude that causes some churches to stay out councils of churches because they consider the member churches as not doctrinally pure, and hopelessly handicapped by antiquated traditions and structures.

However, I personally value tremendously membership of the local council of churches. I see it as an opportunity to put forward the point of view and vision of my own church while at the same time listening to and respecting those of the other member churches. It seems to me to be an invaluable point of contact with other Christians in the neighbourhood. Its value surely depends on what one makes of the opportunity. It is amazing what can, in fact, be achieved through local councils of churches, as we shall see in the next chapter. Obviously, if the council as a whole were to put out a statement or do something that seemed grossly heretical or unChristian, there would be a reason for withdrawing from membership. But in practice, how often would such a thing occur?

It is my firm belief that every local church should join the local council of churches, if one exists. When establishing our church, the Fellowship of the King, in local 'Community church' congregations in the parts of Bristol where we live, we have made joining the churches' council a matter of policy. When we first applied, I expected that we would be rejected and made to feel like sectarian upstarts. In fact, the reverse has been the case. Our applications have never been refused, and we have always been warmly welcomed. Such was the trust we inspired that within a short time of joining, my colleague Dave had become the secretary of one council, and I had become the chairman of another!

There are four good reasons for a church joining their local council of churches. First, each church represents a unique strand of Christianity. For example, my own church is part of a movement that is already significant and fast-growing in England, i.e. the House Churches. House Churches have so much to contribute that I believe it is vital that we, like all other churches, do join churches' councils wherever possible. Equally, we have things to learn and receive from more traditional churches. Second, we share a common concern with all the member churches for the area where we live. Even though our approaches may be different, it is

153

important to listen to one another. We may well learn from other people's insights. Third, we can affect the churches' general policy by the contribution we make. For example, my church has a concern for neighbourhood outreach through such methods as door-to-door visiting and open-air evangelism (with guitars, drama, preaching with a sketchboard, and personal testimony). We hope to be able to use our experience of these methods to help the other churches plan a period of outreach to the neighbourhood. Finally, by meeting together we get to know one another a little. Friendships begin to form. We meet in the street and stop to chat. In this way, those personal contacts are built up which can lead to closer relationships in the family of God.

For church leaders, it's equally important that we attend the local ministers' fraternal. In my own, we meet over lunch, and this is a good opportunity to relax and chat about things in general, building relationships, as well as getting on with the business in hand. We also recently spent a day together to talk, pray, and study the Bible together. Considering that we come from very different backgrounds and theological positions, we found a surprising degree of unity.

In some neighbourhoods, relationships between the churches are so good that they actually covenant with one another to work, worship and witness together as far as possible. Such formalised groupings of local churches are known as Local Ecumenical Projects (LEPs). They have to be approved by the appropriate denominational authorities as well as by the governing bodies of each participating church. Some LEPs only involve two churches (in Bristol, invariably Anglican and Methodist). Others have a wide and exciting variety, e.g. in West Swindon, where Anglicans, Methodists, Roman Catholics, Baptists and United Reformed are included. Ideally, LEPs are, like marriage, the logical culmination of an already excellent relationship. Equally, like marriage, they have to be worked at! They can conveniently provide the structure for all sorts of joint ventures of the type that will be described in the next two chapters, which the leaders will want to initiate if they are listening to God.

Another very important structure which exists to promote unity is the *City Council of Churches*. This works at an intermediate level between the BCC and the local councils. In Bristol, the Greater Bristol Ecumenical Council (GBEC) consists of the denominational leaders (e.g. the Anglican and RC bishops, the Methodist chairman, etc.) and meets three times a year. It is not an elected council with authority to make decisions. Its recommendations have to be ratified by the various denominations involved, using their own methods of decision-making.

The actual work of GBEC is done by working parties that are intended to cover every aspect of the church's life and mission. The aim is to help the participating denominations to pool their resources. For example, in the area of social responsibility, if one denomination is taking a lead in looking after the homeless, the others will support that work rather than set up something new. Other working parties deal with education, communications (the Anglican Mothers' Union regularly monitors TV programmes), theology, the provision of churches on new housing estates, social and industrial ministry, Christian Aid, and the care and oversight of LEPs. There is a secretary, and a monthly newsletter is sent to every congregation which wants it.

The method of decision-making is described as 'gathering consensus'. The secretary has the task of finding out the views of member churches on a whole range of issues. The churches can opt out of any joint decision or statement if they do not agree with it. GBEC is in the forefront of British ecumenical thinking in taking account of the views and activities of each participating denomination rather than trying to pursue a separate ecumenical course which doesn't really have denominational backing.

Many towns and cities, including Bristol, have a regional branch of the national EA. To be member church, you have to subscribe to the doctrinal basis. This would immediately rule out a number of churches which would find the theology too conservative, or too Protestant. The organisation is city-based, and is an excellent forum for gathering information about what is going on in the city in the evangelical constituency. Missions, conferences, special events and specialist ministries are all fully reported. In Bristol, EA has a voice in local religious broadcasting, and sends an observer to the county education committee.

Member churches of local EAs, like those of the national EA, don't represent denominations, but simply themselves. In fact, EA would probably encourage local churches to think and act individually rather than along denominational lines. A useful contribution that a local EA has to make is to provide a forum of fellowship and discussion for churches which are not members of any local or city-wide council of churches, and which may also be totally independent of any denomination is concerned. Also, since EA includes both charismatic (including Pentecostal) and non-charismatic churches, regionally as well as nationally, there is a determination at meetings not to concentrate on the matters that divide us, but rather on projects that we can share together. Unfortunately, there are always a number of churches which stay aloof even from EA.

However, if the existing structures don't adequately express the sort of unity we're aiming at, we must create new ones. The clearest examples of this occur among charismatics. In many areas up and down the country, churches that have been renewed by a fresh touch of the Holy Spirit have looked for ways of expressing unity across the denominations. A great impetus to this search was given in the early 1970s by *Come Together*, a presentation in words and music which aimed to bring together Christians in a locality to express their unity in worship and prayer.[2] I was involved in the Cambridge *Come Together* – to my great surprise, as musical director/ conductor. At one point in the evening, the congregation was encouraged to 'greet somebody in Jesus' name'. This was the signal for everyone to turn to their neighbour and greet them warmly (in many cases, with a hug). As an Anglican, I remember feeling that this was what the offering of 'peace' at Communion really ought to be like. Later in the presentation, we split into groups to pray for one another. At another point, there was a simple statement of the gospel, and an appeal was made to any non-Christians present to commit their lives to Jesus.

Though mildly charismatic (there was a possibility of congregational 'singing in tongues' at one point, and hand-clapping and arm-raising were encouraged), *Come Together* appealed to a wide range of Christians. Enormously popular and effective, it was performed all over the country, in halls, churches and cathedrals (I took part in one particularly impressive performance in Canterbury cathedral). Each local team (choir, band, soloists, narrator/preacher, administrator, spiritual director, and so on) was drawn from a wide variety of denominations. The congregation/audience consisted of members from all the local churches, including Roman Catholics.

A great deal of prayer as well as work went into *Come Together*, and it bore much fruit in growing friendship and goodwill between the churches, as well as conversions and recommitments. There has been nothing quite like it since. It was used by God in a very special way that hasn't ever, perhaps, been fully acknowledged. It created a longing in Christians to continue to meet and worship together. Out of it has come a general movement towards what are often called 'Celebrations': large-scale meetings of several hundred Christians, drawn from many local churches. These would usually start with a relaxed and enthusiastic time of worship, using mainly the new praise songs coming from the House Church movement. This would be followed by an address, often given by someone who is a nationally recognised figure in 'renewal' circles, e.g. Roger Forster, David Pawson, Clifford Hill or Arthur Wallis.

In Bristol, where Celebration meetings have built

157

up from very small beginnings in the late 1970s, they have had the threefold function of 'open praise and worship, preaching, and fellowship'. The aim of Bristol Celebration, stated on every publicity leaflet, is as follows: 'The Celebration Evening is an occasional coming together of God's people from in and around the city. It is an open evening of worship with an invitation to all believers whatever their denominational background to declare together that Jesus Christ is Lord.' The element of fellowship is provided often by a short time of greeting one another, or a time of prayer in groups (as in *Come Together*). As for the preaching, it has always been felt that this should have a prophetic dimension, i.e. the speaker would bring a particular 'word in season' to Christians in Bristol which we need to hear and respond to.

These large central Celebrations are planned and led by a core group of church leaders, which includes two Anglicans, one ordained and one lay, one Baptist and two Pentecostal ministers, two Brethren leaders, and three House Church leaders (including myself). We could all be described as charismatic, and we are united in our desire to allow gifts of the Holy Spirit such as prophecy and healing, to be used at Celebrations if this is appropriate.

Over the last two years, we have sensed something of a change of direction. The Celebrations were in danger of becoming merely rallies for enthusiastic Christians. Meetings that were meant to bring together Christians from the city and its immediate area were attracting people from up to forty miles away. As a result, we felt that we should have a fallow year to take stock. During 1987, we discontinued the Celebrations, but continued to meet in order to talk and pray, trying to sense God's will for future developments. We felt the need to develop in certain directions. We reaffirmed that Celebration was essentially for the churches of Bristol and the small towns and villages in the *immediate vicinity*. This showed that we all accepted the principle of the city church. We saw the need to make occasional public statements relating to *social and moral issues.* We circulated two letters to all local ministers, one on the subject of abortion and the other commenting on the ease of obtaining a divorce in the courts. We asked them to sign the letters if they agreed with the contents, and then sent them to the medical and legal authorities. We also felt that the element of *intercessory prayer* should be incorporated into the large meetings on a more regular basis. Finally, we decided to make *evangelism* a regular feature of Celebration evenings. By the end of 1988 we felt ready to restart the central Celebrations.

Meanwhile, Celebration evenings continued, but on a different basis. In addition to the central meetings, smaller-scale Celebrations have been developing over the past five years in seven areas in and around Bristol. These have played an important role in drawing Christians together in gatherings of 100 to 200, where it is possible to pray with a good deal of common concern for the neighbourhood, and where the element of fellowship plays a more obvious part, as Christians meet, chat over coffee, and pray for one another after the formal part of the evening has finished.

Bristol Celebration is typical of many other similar meetings up and down the country. The desire among Christians to meet for shared free worship, ministry from gifted preachers, and fellowship has been growing for the last decade, and the Celebrations have met this need.

In the search for unity, Christians should take the New Testament concept of the church in the locality much more seriously. David Lillie comments, 'In the strategy of the Holy Spirit for renewal it is the local church which has the key role.'[3] Councils of churches, EAs and Celebrations all provide structures for expressing unity at a local level. Rather than remaining aloof from them or regarding them as a waste of time, we ought to be seeing how God can use them to bring his kingdom in.

Chapter 11

Evangelism and 'Jesus Action'

One thing that the first Christians had in common was the 'Great Commission', Jesus' command to evangelise the nations. This was so important that it occurs, in different forms, in all four gospels and in Acts, where we read the account of how the church began to fulfil it. This was usually done in three stages. First, an apostle or evangelist preached the gospel. Peter at Pentecost is the earliest example of this. He preached under such an anointing of the Spirit that the results were sensational: 3,000 converted on that one occasion. Next, God 'added to their number' (Acts 2.47). This happened because the Church was functioning as it should. A church which exhibits all the features discribed in Acts chapter 2, verses 42 to 47, won't have any difficulty in growing. Finally, every individual Christian preached the Gospel. This happened as a result of persecution: 'Those who had been scattered preached the Word wherever they went' (Acts 8.4). This was probably what we would call 'personal evangelism', i.e. one-to-one sharing of the gospel. It had tremendous results, e.g. the establishment of the church in Antioch, the first to include Gentiles (Acts 11.19–21).

Each of these methods of evangelism is still vitally important in God's plan for world evangelisation mentioned by Jesus in his teaching on the 'end times', when he prophesied, 'This Gospel of the kingdom will be preached in the whole world as a testimony to all nations, and then the end will come' (Matt. 24.14). In other words, one of the few preconditions of the Second Coming of Jesus is that the Gospel should first be preached to every nation. Each generation has to respond afresh to that challenge.[1] In our generation, we in the West are only beginning to grasp the magnitude of the task that faces the Church, while seeing God's Spirit causing people to respond to the Gospel in their thousands in the developing countries. Church growth in South and Central America, sub-Saharan Africa and much of Asia (particularly Korea and China) is phenomenal, and by now well-documented. Europe lags behind the rest of the world, apart from the Islamic countries. Our culture has become post-Christian, heavily secularised. On the one hand, we seem to have become rationalistic, with no room for the supernatural in our way of thinking. Yet on the other hand, the decline of Christianity has left a spiritual vacuum, and strange things have rushed in to fill it. Britain today is riddled with superstition and the occult (witness the popularity of astrology and spiritualism) and increasingly affected by 'New Age' cults as well as the other world religions, which are now an established part of our society. If Christianity is again to flourish in England, where an estimated 90 per cent of the population now have no church connection at all, the Church will have to preach the Gospel to the unconverted in the power of the Holy Spirit using every means at its disposal.

A common concern for evangelism draws Christians together in a remarkable way. Deep in our hearts, there is a desire to see the lost saved, and those who are living sub-standard lives released into the joy and liberty of following Christ. We want others to share what we ourselves know and experience of God's goodness.

Another factor in the life of the early church which can powerfully unite Christians is a concern for the poor and needy. Jesus told the parable of the Good Samaritan to show that God can give his people a love for their needy neighbour which transcends even the most colossal man-made social barriers, like the one which existed between Jews and Samaritans in the first century. The early Christians worked out this concern initially within the local church. The Jerusalem community shared their resources so that the needy were fed and clothed. Later, when that church faced famine, Paul organised a collection for them from among the other churches on the simple principle of equality: 'At the present time

161

your plenty will supply what they need, so that in turn their plenty will supply what you need. Then there will be equality' (II Cor. 8.14). But this generosity easily spilled out beyond the confines of the church into the world; so Paul wrote, 'As we have opportunity, let us do good to all people' (Gal. 6.10).

Concern for the poor, sick and needy does wonderfully draw Christians together in works of compassion. But in this we would be no different from a group of concerned humanists except for the fact that it is God who is setting the agenda for us, giving us his priorities, his love and his resources. Today, Christians in Britain are so used to secular agencies doing works of charity which in the past would probably have been done by the church that we refer to our own initiatives simply as 'social action', and we speak of 'the social gospel' when describing this aspect of the church's work. But it would be more honouring to God to use the phrase 'Jesus action' (coined in the London-based 'Ichthus Christian Fellowship'), for it is the love of Jesus that inspires his people to do these works of love.

In that sense, evangelism and Jesus action are two sides of the same coin. Both spring out of a love for God and for our neighbour. We share the gospel because we love God for what he has done for us, and because he has given us such love for others that we want them too to enter into a relationship with him. His love within us also gives us compassion for our fellow human beings, and so we are moved by the Holy Spirit to serve and minister to others. It is a strategy of the devil to divide evangelism and Jesus action. They are intimately related.

For example, if a team of Christians are doing house-to-house visiting in their neighbourhood to share the good news about Jesus, they will meet a few people who actually want to talk about God. Some of these will be genuinely seeking him, and may come to a point of commitment. But if they do, they will bring a whole bundle of needs, problems and hurts into the kingdom with them, and these will have to be sorted out through practical love and care within the church family. The visitors will also meet people who only want to talk about their needs, and who desperately want help. In the course of helping them, the Christians may well have an opportunity to share the gospel and lead them to Christ. So it is impossible for the gospel proclamation to be divorced from its practical outworking. As James writes in his letter, 'faith by itself, if it is not accompanied by action, is dead' (James 2.17).

I want in the remainder of this chapter to look at some examples of how God has used a common concern for evangelism and Jesus action to draw Christians together and create some degree of unity between them. Many of these examples are taken from the Bristol area, but they can be paralleled many times over in other parts of the country.

First, *evangelism.* I have twice been involved in large-scale evangelistic campaigns in Bristol. The first, in 1982, was a 'Down to Earth' mission led by Eric Delve. This took place in three areas of the city – two local, and one central and easily accessible to all. The time of mission itself (about a month) was a success, in that more than 100 people committed or recommitted their lives to Christ. Only a small number of churches were involved in supporting the mission, but those that were gave themselves to the task enthusiastically. Ours was one of them, and I was personally involved on the organising committee. As a group, we were closely drawn together as we prepared for the mission (we met once a month for several months). But because we represented churches scattered all over a city of some 500,000 people, there was no way we could cement that unity after the mission period was over. My impression is that, on the whole, any unity established between local churches through 'Down to Earth' has not lasted. There are probably three main reasons for this. Not all the churches participated. Those that did were not as committed to the mission as they might have been. Finally, it was not followed up by an ongoing programme of joint outreach in the areas concerned.

The next, much larger, campaign of this sort was

more effective on all counts. 'Mission England', a process which lasted for three years (1982–5), had as its centrepiece Billy Graham's visit to England in the late spring and summer of 1984. It was on a vast scale compared with 'Down to Earth'. Bristol was the centre of the entire south-west region, with the organising office situated here. Because of the high profile given by its backers (the EA) to Billy Graham's visit, and because of the very thorough nationwide preparation for it, spanning two years, a large proportion of churches within each regional catchment area were involved – particularly in the centres where the stadium meetings were actually to take place (e.g. Bristol). As a result, a high degree of local unity was felt between the participating churches. For example, training for counselling new converts at the stadium, and for leading home-based 'nurture groups' afterwards, took part to a certain extent on an area basis within the city, and members of different local churches met and mingled at these sessions. There was a strong sense of being 'one in spirit and purpose' (Phil. 2.2). Also, because a very large number of churches in the Bristol area were actively involved, each one of us felt part of an army, united in playing our part in the great campaign. As the preparations built up, I began to realise in amazement just how many churches and individual Christians had devoted prayer, time, money and expertise towards our common goal.

The week of the stadium meetings at Ashton Gate football ground was clearly the climax of Mission England in the south west. With an average nightly attendance of around 30,000, and 20,444 enquirers to follow up in the whole region (of whom about a half were from Bristol), the sheer scale of the proceedings gave a sense of a church united in proclaiming the gospel to the region and, indeed, to the nation. Many Christians were on a spiritual 'high' for weeks afterwards. The results were clear. Several thousand new converts were added to the church, while many Christians whose faith had become lukewarm rededicated themselves to Christ. The city, and the nation (Dr Graham subsquently preached in five other cities), became aware of the importance and the power of the undiluted Gospel.

What has all this done to encourage Christian unity in Bristol? First, at least one important city-wide ministry has developed out of Mission England which expresses both evangelism and Jesus action, and which is drawing together Christians from many different church backgrounds: 'Network', a Christian counselling service. Second, a certain amount of goodwill has been established between the participating churches, on an area basis. This is difficult to quantify; it's a subtle change of atmosphere. Finally, and probably most importantly, bonds of relationship and friendship have been formed and strengthened between individual Christians who worked and prayed together over a long period of time. The stadium stewarding team, for example, who had the difficult job of marshalling the enormous crowds, developed such a spirit of fellowship and dedication that they were willing to chase over the country helping at subsequent meetings where there was a lack of stewards, and they have been acting as stewards for Celebration ever since.

My own feeling is that evangelism best expresses and fosters Christian unity if it is *area-based* and *ongoing*. Although I see the need for large-scale evangelism, particularly as a catalyst for individual churches to 'get on with it', it seems to me that the most effective form of evangelism is plainer, humbler, and less spectacular, but may be infinitely more exciting. After the big campaign, once the gifted evangelist has packed his bags and gone, the local church members have the talk of proclaiming the good news, week in and week out, in the areas where they live. Such united evangelism needs to be *area-based* to target the specific needs of the neighbourhood, and to include the maximum number of local churches. It needs to be *ongoing* in order that the relationships of love and trust that are forming may grow more committed.

The best potential forum for joint evangelism in an area is undoubtedly the local council of churches. For it to function effectively, however, there must be enough churches, or at any rate enough individual representatives of the council, who see the need and have the vision. There must also be sufficient strongly-motivated church members to form an evangelism sub-committee and bring the vision into reality. A friend of mine, who is chairman of the evangelism sub-committee of his council of churches in the Guildford area, recently described to me the programme of joint evangelism that they had devised. In the summer 1988, there was a 'Make Way' march through the town centre, in which all the churches participated. This was the prelude to a series of eight seminars in 1989, which consisted of a basic introduction to the whole subject of evangelism, followed by sessions on evangelism at work, reaching men, reaching women, 'lifestyle evangelism', the tools of evangelism (e.g. literature, videos, etc.), street theatre and mime, and open-air work. These seminars were led by nationally recognised teachers. They were followed by a period of outreach later in the year, when individual churches 'did their own thing'. That seems the one disappointing feature of an exciting joint venture. It would have been really good if the outreach to the town could have been shared in the same way as the training that led up to it.

That particular council of churches consists of twenty churches, of which slightly more than half could be considered 'evangelical'. They have been able to plan and carry out a powerful joint act of witness, and an imaginative programme of evangelistic training. This shows that inter-church structures are there to be used in the work of God. It simply takes a few people with vision and energy and a belief in the power of prayer to get on and use the opportunity in a creative way.

The most remarkable example of unity through evangelism that I know of took place in 1987 in a town of about 15,000 inhabitants near Bristol which I shall simply call 'Littletown' (the leaders prefer not to be identified as they say that their unity is far from perfect, and don't want to appear as anything special!). Littletown, which includes rapidly growing housing developments, has thirteen churches – all the main denominations, plus four small House Churches formed from various splits. Until the early 1980s, relations between the churches had been cool. Then, within a short time, most of the leaders were replaced. The new leaders made a real effort to build bridges, and friendly relationships developed between them. In particular, the two Anglican ministers shared a similar vision for Church growth in the love and power of the Holy Spirit. The Roman Catholic priest was also very sympathetic to their approach. One of the vicars encouraged the House Churches to join the town's council of churches – which, surprisingly, they did.

Early in January 1985, John, the other Anglican vicar, became chairman of the council, and shared his powerful vision for joint outreach to the town. He encouraged the representatives of the churches to take his ideas back to their fellowships for prayer and discussion. A year later, the 'Littletown Jesus Festival' was launched. It was proposed by the Brethren, and seconded by the Roman Catholics! It was decided that each church would sponsor its own outreach events during a fifteen-month period. To plan a final joint week of outreach, a working group was appointed under John's chairmanship consisting of one representative from each church. John asked that they should be released from any other main responsibility in their church. This was predominantly, but not entirely, a charismatic/evangelical group, so it is interesting that they decided not to adopt a formal joint statement of faith for the festival. They felt that as they could each say sincerely 'Jesus is Lord', that was enough. The group started meeting weekly in September; the joint week of outreach which was the climax of the festival took place the following May. Half of the meeting was taken up with prayer, and no decisions were made that did not come out of their praying together. A hundred people met in neighbourhood-based inter-church prayer triplets, following the pattern of Mission England. A worship group started to meet

167

weekly to rehearse a musical/dramatic presentation based on the book of Ruth, written by one of the local doctors.

Some aspects of this outreach were decidedly unconventional. For example, the budget was set early on at about £20,000, but the working group decided against asking each church for a contribution. Instead, they felt that every penny should simply be 'prayed in'. It was! They also decided to give away 10 per cent of all income to missions or Christian charities as soon as it came in. The venue for the main meetings was also unusual: a derelict garage, converted to hold 550 people, it was redecorated, relit, and fitted with tiered seating for the choir. This major task was achieved by voluntary labour from the churches. Inevitably, it brought Christians together as never before. The main week of mission included continuous reading of Scripture in the shopping precinct from nine a.m. to five p.m., interspersed with open-air evangelism and drama. The evening meetings were short, concentrating on a gospel message brought by a visiting speaker. A team of local Christians visited all the schools, taking assemblies and RE lessons.

As a result of the festival week, 100 converts were made, but the main effect was a tough and unexpected challenge to the (by then) much more united churches of Littletown. The visiting evangelist spoke of their lack of commitment, and of their being ready to settle for what they had got, i.e. a comfortable and materialistic Christianity that dodged the cost of discipleship. Since then, the leaders have addressed themselves to the differences that still separate them. Tensions have been revealed between the evangelical/charismatics, in the majority, and the more liberal Christians, who lay less stress on evangelism and more on community care. Some leaders have felt the need to spend more time, for the present, building up their own congregations than on inter-church events. None the less, things in Littletown will never be quite the same again. A survey has shown that, in the year of outreach culminating in the main Jesus Festival week, the number of churchgoers in Littletown doubled from 10 per cent to 20 per cent of the population – twice the national average.

The part that prayer played in the preparation for the Jesus Festival was significant. Concerned Christians had been praying on a regular weekly basis for reconciliation between the churches for several years before a joint outreach was ever thought of. Also, a group of clergy and Christian doctors (Littletown has two Christian practices) had been meeting every Wednesday morning to pray. The link between effective outreach and prayer cannot be too highly emphasised.

Turning now to Jesus Action, we need to remember that evangelism and Jesus Action are in fact two sides of the same coin. A good example of how joint evangelism can give rise to joint community care is given by 'Network', a Christian counselling service based in Bristol. This was conceived during the period leading up to the stadium meetings of Mission England, when a committee was formed to discuss ways of both advertising the mission, and giving an opportunity for Bristolians to talk in confidence about any religious questions or other personal problems that they might have. Training in counselling was given by 'Scope Ministries', which is based in the USA and works closely with the Billy Graham Organisation. It was decided to park a caravan in the main Bristol shopping-centre which would be a dropping-in point for any interested passers-by.

The person in charge of organising this ministry was David Mitchell, a Bristol solicitor who, with his wife Christine, was already leading 'Marriage Repair', a Christian marriage guidance counselling service in the city. After the stadium meetings were over, and the immediate excitement of Mission England had died down, David and Christine felt strongly led to link Marriage Repair with the Mission England structure and develop a new Christian counselling service dealing with the full range of personal problems, using the insights and teaching given by Scope Ministries. In this way, Network was born, and has developed from small

169

beginnings into a city-wide ministry which now not only helps 400 people every year, but also trains its own counsellors, organises specialist seminars on subjects ranging from anorexia to deliverance ministry, and lays on courses for churches which request training for their own pastoral teams.

Network has been a powerful means of drawing together Christians from many varied backgrounds. Counsellors come from twenty-five different churches, clients from a far greater number, including some which have well-developed counselling ministries of their own. Most of the counsellors could be described as evangelical (although one is an RC nun, and some of the seminar speakers are also Catholics), and have to give an account of their own personal faith as part of the selection procedure, but they represent a spectrum of belief embracing both charismatic and non-charismatic. To some extent, this affects the allocation of client to counsellor (it is helpful to link like with like), but it does not cause any problem of relationship within the counselling team. Members of all the main denominations are involved in one way or another.

The present director of Network, John Turner, is no stranger to the concept of Christian unity expressed through joint community care. When he lived in the Greater Manchester area thirteen years ago, he led a ministry involving three local churches which provided, not formalised counselling, but practical care for the community. Various specialist groups were set up, including a visiting team, a transport group, an odd-jobs brigade, emergency help with legal and tax matters, and a support prayer group. Fuses were mended, coal was humped, an elderly couple were driven to their holiday destination. Such shared ministry drew the Christians together, and denominational differences were forgotten. An important part of the ministry was that each group met regularly to pray together about their work. That sort of model is one which a local council of churches could do well to consider adopting, if they had a vision for shared community care. I know of another scheme in Durham where the council of churches runs a community health project for those suffering from schizophrenia.

In Bristol, most joint Jesus Action seems to follow the Network model, i.e. that of a specialist ministry dependent on the vision of one person or a small group, but relying on the support of many different churches and individual Christians. Other ministries of this sort in Bristol include the night shelter run by the Julian Trust, which caters for those who would normally sleep rough, providing a bed, evening meal and breakfast; and the Missing Peace coffee shop, which ministers particularly to those with drug-related problems. The latter has a strong evangelistic flavour, in that it sees the ultimate solution to such problems as a life-changing relationship with Jesus Christ, and actually sends teams out onto the streets to chat to people and invite them to the shop.

Perhaps the most dramatic development of this kind, which certainly made the headlines in the local media, has been the 'Caring at Christmas' project. In 1987, Ron Smith, an assistant diocesan secretary in the Bristol Anglican Diocese, had the vision of offering 24-hour food, accommodation, entertainment, fellowship and a relaxed Christmas atmosphere for five days over the Christmas period for those who were sleeping rough. Once the project was publicised, the response from the churches and from the public at large was phenomenal. A redundant Anglican church and church hall were made available for accommodation. At a meeting called for volunteers, 600 people turned up, and had to queue to get in. Helpers came from as far afield as Dorset, Wales and Somerset. There was an overwhelming response to an appeal for clothes, and another redundant church was used as a store. Televisions, entertainment, a medical team, and hair-dressers, as well as the clothing store, were all provided free. The council set up a shower cabin, which was very much appreciated, and well used!

Goods flooded in. Dustbins, brushes, pork-pies and sausages were all provided free. The Mothers' Union baked 3,500 mince pies. Finally, 1,497 tins of soup appeared, catering size, with eighty-eight servings in each – kindly provided by a well-known manufacturer. So much money was donated that Ron was able to refit the ageing church hall kitchens with a large cooker, new hot-water system, toaster, kitchen units and sinks, and new plumbing. On Christmas Day, eighty-four were catered for. A local chemist organised free supplies of medicine, and heads were deloused. No alcohol was allowed on the premises, and a happy, peaceful atmosphere prevailed. Caring at Christmas is continuing; during the rest of the year, the refurbished premises are being used regularly by the Night Shelter.

It is clear from the examples that I have given that it is perfectly possible for churches in a locality to work together in evangelism and Jesus Action. Such co-operation can be in the context of an already existing structure, usually a council of churches, local branch of EA, or Celebration–style group, or through a new ministry raised up by God for a particular purpose. Depending on the grouping, it may well be appropriate to base such shared activity on a common statement of faith. On the other hand, it may be adequate simply to affirm together that 'Jesus is Lord'. In the case of Jesus Action, it could well be appropriate to accept the help and support of non-Christian volunteers, as long as the leadership and general direction of operations lies in the hands of Christians, as is the case with Caring at Christmas. If Jesus used the example of a good Samaritan to teach true neighbourliness, he would hardly reject a non-Christian who wants to lend a hand in a Christian ministry of caring.

There are sincere Christians, I know, who would find it impossible to co-operate in this way with Roman Catholics and, probably, with liberal churches. The danger here is of isolationalism. If we are to work together, we cannot wait until we are in total theological agreement with one another. Nor will it do to state that evangelicals can work with one another, but not with Catholics, liberals, and those in 'mixed' denominations.

Immediately, you deny the tremendous potential and richly diverse contribution of Christians in the non-evangelical churches. The vexed question of placing new converts in appropriate churches usually turns out to be a non-problem, as most people are converted through contact with a Christian friend, and would therefore naturally attend the friend's church, at any rate to start off with. As for converts with no church links, we should trust that God will lead them to join the church where they will receive the most help.

Working together in this way will certainly not always be easy, but it will be a vital learning and growing experience for all concerned. With God's help, everyone's horizons will greatly expand. Most important of all, his kingdom will begin to have an impact on society as the Gospel is proclaimed in words, works and (increasingly) wonders, and many are converted.

Chapter 12

Prayer and Revival

We have seen how God can establish unity between his people as they join together to bring Christ to a needy world. More important than this for unity, however, is the relationship with God which all Christians share. *Prayer* is the most fundamental and important activity which we can engage in together. *Revival*, God's sovereign transformation of the church by an outpouring of his spirit, is not so much a Christian activity as a possible future event that we should be praying for with all the zeal and perseverance that we can muster. If the will for unity is already present in the church, revival will bring it to pass swiftly and dynamically.

We saw Chapter 3 that *prayer* is at the very heart of Christian unity. It establishes our vertical unity with God. This is true individually and collectively. When a church needs to make an important decision, it is vital that the members come together in the presence of God to seek to know his will on the matter. Many churches make decisions on the basis of the majority vote of representatives elected to a church council. At best, this is done prayerfully and carefully, and as a method it does have the merit of allowing for disagreement and minority views to be expressed. It doesn't, however, seem ideal. Collective decision-making under the leading of the Holy Spirit of God should have a sense of rightness about it that causes everyone present to agree. A vote should never be necessary. Time and again I have observed this in the leadership meetings of our own church. We have strong personalities and often stubbornly-held views. But we find that as we wait on God, alternately discussing and praying, we are led into a unity of spirit that seemed at first impossible to achieve.

Collective prayer can, in fact, provide the perfect opportunity for God to speak powerfully into a situation, thus enabling a creative and important decision to be made. A good example of this is the decision made by the leaders of the Antioch church to send Barnabas and Saul on their first missionary journey (Acts 13.1–3). It was while they were worshipping the Lord and fasting that the Holy Spirit clearly spoke, presumably through a word of prophecy given by one of those present, tested and accepted by the others: 'Set apart for me Barnabas and Saul for the work to which I have called them' (v.2). Those words were to prove vital for the next stage of development of the whole church.

Since many House Churches have been criticised as authoritarian in the way they make decisions, it may be of interest to explain how the process works in our own church. Usually, God speaks to one of the leaders individually in prayer about some new development – the setting up of an evangelism team, for example. He or she then shares this with the rest of the leadership group for their testing. If, after further thought, discussion and prayer, we sense that we have the mind of the Lord, we put the plan forward to the church as a suggestion. It is then up to each member of the church individually to pray about it, weigh it, and respond positively or negatively. The matter may also be discussed in the home groups. On the basis of the response we get, the leaders then proceed to implement the plan, with a confident sense that we have achieved unity of heart and purpose. If there were a strong negative response, we would certainly get back to the drawing board, and to further prayer. We are, incidentally, very open to suggestions about future developments coming from non-leaders, and we always consider them very carefully if they have clearly been made on the basis of prayer and a revelation from God, and in the right positive spirit.[1]

However, collective prayer does not simply have to do with decision-making. Two even more important areas of prayer relating to unity which we must consider are *intercession* and *repentance*. In *intercession*, we pray on behalf of someone else. Abraham interceded for the people of Sodom, pleading with God not to destroy the city if there were only ten righteous people left in it

(Genesis 18.22–33). Moses interceded for the Israelites as they fought the Amalekites, his hands held up by Aaron and Hur (Exodus 17.10–13). Jesus interceded for his people after the Last Supper (John 17), and he 'always lives to intercede for them' (Hebrews 7.25). Paul intercedes for the Ephesians that 'you may be filled to the measure of all the fulness of God' (Eph. 3.19).

Intercession should play an important part in our prayers as individuals. It is hard work, because it does often involve wrestling with God, discovering his mind and heart in the actual process of praying. It also involves sensing in the spirit the needs of the person you are praying for, and the way in which God intends to satisfy them. Answers to this type of prayer are rarely instantaneous. God tests our stickability, and thereby draws out of us faith and perseverance.

Intercession as a group activity involves far more than the 'shopping list' type of prayer meeting in which each person prays for the topic that is on their heart without listening to what their neighbour is praying. To be an effective intercession group, we have to probe the purposes of God. The topics for prayer have to be selected according to his agenda, and the prayer must proceed along the lines dictated by his Spirit. As we pray, we need to be sensitive to his word to us, coming through prophecy, visions, Scripture or any other means of revelation. I have found myself doing strange things at intercession meetings! Recently, a group of us praying for Bristol felt moved to blow onto a map of the city in order prophetically to symbolise the Holy Spirit breathing new life into dead structures. None of us would rationally have decided to do such a thing; the Spirit clearly guided us. We also have to learn to concentrate on the topic in hand, and not to move onto another topic until the first one has been prayed about adequately. In other words, we need to have a sense as a group that we have 'prayed through' each topic as far as God intends on any particular occasion. Once that has happened, we can move on to a new topic.

Pioneers in this type of prayer nationally have been

the Lydia Prayer Fellowship, groups of Christian women who intercede about local, national and international affairs, and Intercessors for Britain, who concentrate on prayer for the nation. Recently, there have been moves organised on a more local basis to pray for towns and cities, and these have brought together Christians from many different churches. In Bristol, for example, a group of about thirty Christians started meeting in conjunction with Celebration to pray regularly once a month for the city. It was given considerable impetus during Mission England, but after several years, it felt that its work was done, and that God wanted a new initiative to be taken.

At about the same time, Clifford Hill and a small team came to the city and spoke of the need for a coming together of leaders for prayer. Various developments have arisen from this. Leaders have met several times for mornings of prayer for the city. In addition, a smaller group of folk drawn from a number of churches met every week for six months to pray for the city. One of the city-wide Celebrations was specifically devoted to the subject of intercession, particularly with the city in mind, with Arthur Wallis as the speaker. At that meeting an appeal was given for all those who felt called to intercede for the city on a regular basis to give their names and addresses to the stewards. About 175 people responded, and out of these eight prayer groups were formed on an area basis to pray not simply for the city but for particular localities within it. The original small group split up at this point, many of its members becoming the leaders of the new groups.

Each group has been free to decide its own time, place and frequency of meeting. Some have opted to meet monthly, others fortnightly, others weekly. Two groups are meeting weekly at six-thirty a.m., as this is clearly the most convenient time to get everyone together. In fact, there is a lot to be said for early-morning prayer meetings, provided that people are reasonably awake. One's mind is not yet cluttered by the concerns of the day, and the sense of freshness can inspire even the sleepiest meeting. The only real problem with an early time is that it might crowd out the individual prayer times of the group members, which would be a pity. For an intercession group to be really successful, it needs to be made up of people who are intercessors on their own, not just in the group.

As an expression of Christian unity, an inter-church intercession group inevitably presents greater problems than one based entirely on a single local church. There is the fact that group members often don't know each other very well. A common occurrence in any prayer group is that one person may have a tendency to highlight their own personal problems, thus causing the group prayer to focus on themselves. In a church prayer group, this can relatively easily be dealt with, as the leader will be well aware of the problem. In an inter-church group, it will take time for the situation to emerge, and the group leader will have to use great sensitivity in speaking to the person concerned, whom he or she may not know very well.

Then there is the question of the style of prayer and worship of each group member. In the group that I am leading at the moment in our area, this ranges from Pentecostal (with audible and often continuous speaking in tongues, loud 'Amens', and hand-clapping) to a much more restrained manner. If there is a wide spectrum of prayer styles in the group, problems may ensue. One style will tend to swamp the others, and people will probably feel upset. In these circumstances, it is vital that the group leader brings the problem out into the open for discussion. If this is done in the right spirit, the group will be able to find its own unique way of praying, where folk both accept one another's traditions and also modify their own style out of love for one another. In this way, true unity will be established within the group. The most important thing is that there should be a flow of prayer in the Spirit. This is possible despite different styles of prayer within the same group.

However great the problems posed by an inter-church intercession group, the blessings far outweigh them. In our group, for example, there is a sense of the Lord's love drawing together Pentecostals, Anglicans, Baptists, and members of independent fellowships. We know that we are united through our common faith in Christ as well as our shared concern for the city, and this enables us to pray together in harmony, despite our very different prayer traditions.

One important aspect of prayer which any intercession group worth its salt will inevitably be drawn into is *spiritual warfare*. A potent factor that will bind together a group drawn from different churches is the sense that we are allies fighting a common enemy. In this fight, our unity is essential. 'Unity is another indispensable spiritual weapon with which the Church must be equipped if it is to make any significant inroads into the realm of Satan', wrote Michael Green.[2] God will reveal to .his praying people the strongholds of Satan, and direct us to pray against them in specific ways. Such prayer may have to be backed up by action. A good example of this is the stand taken in 1986–7 by Ichthus Christian Fellowship in South London against the policies of Lewisham Borough Council in positively promoting homosexuality. Ichthus not only mobilised prayer support among twenty-six local churches, but leafleted 80,000 homes in the area with a statement signed by these churches, and confronted council leaders in private debate.

In our own local intercession group for the city, we felt led to pray against a local witches' coven. We turned in the direction of the area where the coven meets, and began to praise God with great fervour. Then we took authority over the powers of darkness, declaring them powerless in the name of Jesus. I feel sure that this is the beginning, not the end, of our prayers on this topic, as Satan is deeply entrenched in such centres of occult activity. However, every battle has to start somewhere, and we cannot always tell immediately what effect such prayer has had on the situation. Perhaps the clearest feature of our prayer was the instant unity we all felt as Christians in the face of the presence of a monstrous evil.

An increasing amount of prayer is going on at the

moment for local government. Here too we can sense the presence of enemy forces. A group of church leaders was recently able to pray for Bristol City Council in the very committee room where many of the key policy decisions are made. We had heard from a Christian councillor of the back stabbing and character assassination that went on in the building, and we were overwhelmed by a feeling of spiritual darkness. Once again, we took authority over the evil forces, and claimed the victory of Jesus, praying for every aspect of the council's activities. Christians are increasingly feeling that it is important to go and pray in the actual buildings where important political and social decisions are made. Others walk around the streets, praying outside key buildings. Some follow the line of the medieval walls of a town or city, which symbolises its identity.

The second aspect of prayer that is drawing Christians together at this time is *repentance*. On 5th March, 1988, an event of considerable spiritual significance took place which went largely unnoticed by the media apart from a few Christian publications. For the first time since the Second World War, a *National Day of Repentance* was called. For several years, groups such as Intercessors for Britain and the Lydia Prayer Fellowship have been faithfully praying for the nation. Scriptures such as II Chronicles chapter 7, verse 14, have long seemed significant to those who have faithfully interceded for Britain: 'If my people, who are called by my name, will humble themselves and pray and seek my face and turn from their wicked ways, then will I hear from heaven and will forgive their sin and will heal their land.' This theme had already been sounded in 1976, when a musical act of worship and prayer called *If My People*, by Jimmy and Carol Owens (the same husband-and-wife team who composed *Come Together*) was performed all over the country.[3] I was personally involved in singing in some performances which took place in Westminster Cathedral in London, and I remember the profound and solemn note that was struck as Christian MPs and peers led prayers of intercession and repentance for the nation. The evening ended with an appeal to people to make a solemn convenant with God to pray for the nation. How many, I wonder, have kept this promise? I know that my own response has been in fits and starts. But as I have seen the spiritual, moral and social decline of our nation in the intervening years, I am more and more convinced of the need of the Church to repent.

There is some controversy regarding the question of whether Christians can repent on behalf of the sins of the nation. Jeremiah chapter 18, verses 7 and 8, which is often quoted in this context, implies that the whole nation has the responsibility for repenting, rather as the whole city of Babylon repents in the book of Jonah (when even the animals fasted – chapter 3, verse 7). In Daniel chapter 9, verses 1 to 19, Daniel certainly identifies himself with and confesses the sin of Israel: 'While I was speaking and praying, confessing my sin and the sin of my people Israel' (v.20). How does this apply to Christians in Britain today?

We must bear in mind that Israel was the people of God. For a Christian, to identify with Israel means primarily to identify with the Church. If our nation is in a mess, it is because the church has failed to preach and live out the gospel faithfully and convincingly. Christians need to repent collectively of such sins within the church as apathy, unbelief, sexual immorality, misuse of money, materialism, heresy and, of course, divisiveness. But I personally also think there is a sense in which we, as British Christians, can acknowledge the guilt of the nation in allowing such things as abortion on demand, gross social injustice, racism and violence to go largely unchecked. We need to identify with our nation's sins. As Brian Mills, until recently the prayer and revival secretary of the EA, has written, 'When we look at the nation . . . we are not in a position to repent on its behalf, but we can confess its wrongs.'[4] What God surely most wants to see in the church is a basic attitude of humility and a determination to turn from what is wrong towards true holiness.

During the Second World War, there was such a sense in the nation that we were fighting against an evil power, such a determination that we must win at all costs, and a generally much higher level of Christian commitment, that it was not difficult for the King and the Prime Minister to call the whole nation to prayer. God certainly granted us some remarkable and unexpected victories.[5] In our generation, in a peacetime situation, we are being attacked by an evil that is *within* the nation. Our slide down the slippery slope into immorality and chaos is gradual and hardly apparent except to those with eyes to see. The most perceptive Christians in this respect are the prophets and the intercessors. It was a coalition of these which called the nation to repentance and prayer on 5th March, 1988. Appeals had been made to the Queen and to the Prime Minister to back the call, but to no avail. Those responsible, then, were the Evangelical Alliance, Care Trust, the Lydia Fellowship, Prophetic Word Ministries (led by Clifford Hill), Action for Biblical Witness to Our Nation (led by Tony Higton, and working mainly within the Church of England), and Intercessors for Britain (the co-ordinators).

IFB estimated that 40–50,000 may have taken part, with approximately 2,000 attending at some stage during the day at Westminster Central Hall, 800 at Newcastle and Southend, and a major meeting in Belfast covering the six counties. In Bristol, several churches held their own meetings in the morning, there was continuous prayer during the day at a central venue, and an inter-church meeting in the evening. It was noticeable that, on the whole, only a small proportion of church members took part. Repentance is not a popular item on the Christian agenda. We would much rather be caught up in worship, or experiencing the signs and wonders of the Holy Spirit. Yet if, as I have suggested, repentance is such a basic part of our daily private prayer, shouldn't it be programmed into our corporate prayer as churches, since we are responsible for the spiritual, moral and social health of the nation? Those who prayed on 5th March, 1988, certainly thought so.

IFB reported that the most overwhelming comment on the day was the need for further occasions of the same sort. They felt that, if we are to see a major breakthrough, we must persist in prayer. This will have to happen by Christians from different churches coming together in cities and towns, united in heart and mind, and determined to pray with humble and repentant hearts until God sends revival to the church and a spiritual awakening to our nation. More days of prayer and repentance are planned.

A *revival* is an outpouring of the Holy Spirit on the Church nationally, regionally or individually as a result of sustained, persevering prayer in a humble attitude of repentance by a significant number of believers. Revivals are initiated by God, and can never be exactly predicted (though prophets may have a clear sense that they are part of God's imminent plan). Characteristics of a revival include a desire for personal and corporate holiness; priority given to intercession by entire churches, e.g. in all-night prayer vigils and periods of fasting; public preaching of the gospel, leading to conversions on a large scale; and miraculous signs and wonders, including healing and deliverance. When a revival significantly affects the life of a nation, historians use the word 'awakening' to describe the resultant phenomenon (as in the name 'the Great Awakening' used to describe what happened in the USA in the mid-1700s).

Revivals are currently in progress in many countries, including Korea, Zaire, Nigeria, Indonesia, Nicaragua and parts of North-East India such as Nagaland. The last to occur in Britain was the Hebridean revival of the early 1950s, which was localised on certain Scottish islands. Before that came the Welsh revival of the 1900s, the effect of which was considerable, but seems largely to have faded. In England, there has been no major revival since the awakening of 1859, of which Spurgeon wrote, 'The times of refreshing from the presence of the Lord have at last dawned upon our land. A spirit of prayer is visiting our churches. The first breath of the rushing mighty wind is already discerned.'[6]

183

A revival does not, however, necessarily bring unity between Christians. Revived churches tend to see themselves as distinct from and superior to those that are not revived. Moreover, even among revived churches, rivalry can persist. In Korea, for example, revival in many of the denominations does not seem to have led to deeper fellowship between them. I suspect that if revival comes about through each church or denomination praying individually, the divisions tend to continue even in the revival. On the other hand, if the churches corporately acknowledge their weakness and sinfulness, and make a point of praying, worshipping and evangelising together, revival tends to draw them even closer to one another. I would hope that, in a true revival in England, the only division would be between those churches (and Christians) who really want to follow Jesus wherever he leads, and those who do not.

A growing number of Christians leaders believe that revival in England – and Britain as a whole – could happen very soon. This, however, is conditional on the faith, prayer and repentance of the church. Clifford Hill is notable among those who have sought both to discern the 'signs of the times', God's warning signs of judgment, and to sound a note of hope if only Christians in Britain will turn back to God. In the already-mentioned article in *Prophecy Today,* which he edits, he writes, 'If Christians are faithful today in turning to God and seeking his forgiveness and pleading for the nation he will answer with the fire of the Holy Spirit. New life and power will sweep across the land and the faithful will rejoice to see the name of Jesus glorified in Britain.'[7] But he also sees clearly that the church in our nation is confronted with a stark choice between revival and disaster. It remains to be seen how the Church will respond to his warnings and exhortations. All prophecy has to be tested, and then acted upon if it is accepted as the word of God. Christians need to pay attention to Clifford Hill.

Another person who is anticipating revival is Bob Dunnett, vice-principal of Birmingham Bible Institute.

He is the leader of the team that organises 'Pray for Birmingham', which came into being in 1986. From the outset, they felt that they had two clear directions from God. First, they were convinced that traditional patterns of intercessory prayer were not right for the present situation. Second, they felt that somehow the new pattern had something to do with the open air. At precisely the same time, the songwriter and worship-leader Graham Kendrick published his *Make Way* presentation, which he designed to do exactly what they envisaged. Both the Birmingham group and Kendrick (from Ichthus Christian Fellowship in London) sought to make 'high praise' a prayer tool. Starting on the south and north sides of Birmingham, a procession of several hundred Christians converged on the city centre praising God and proclaiming the lordship of Jesus using Kendrick's *Make Way* music.

Since then, there have been regular large-scale Make Ways in Birmingham. For example, ten separate groups have simultaneously walked round the thirty-mile-long outer boundary of the city, singing and praying as they went. Marches from different points on the perimeter have converged on the city centre. There has been activity in the suburbs and in the inner city. Each march has been preceded by a half-night of prayer in Birmingham Cathedral lasting four hours, which included praise, intercession both sung and spoken (Dunnett is convinced of the contemporary relevance of sung prayer, e.g. Kendrick's song 'Shine, Jesus, shine'), and teaching. Apparently, the response of young people has been particularly enthusiastic; half of the 1,700 attending the half-nights of prayer are under twenty-two.

Even more significant than Prayer for Birmingham has been the most recent development of Dunnett's team. As they spent days away together seeking direction of God, they heard clearly through a word of prophecy that they were to raise up the banner of revival in the nation as a whole. This is now the core of their vision. For

185

them, revival means, first, the life of the nation deeply influenced by a holy, repentant church, and, second, a major move of the Holy Spirit in the land which will sweep literally hundreds of thousands of people into the kingdom of God.

In order to communicate that vision to a large number of people, Pray for Birmingham adopted the name 'Pray for Revival' and took a bold step of faith in hiring Birmingham's National Exhibition Centre – an expensive venture as it holds 11,000 people. In fact, so great was the response from around Britain that they had to hire an overflow hall as well. On 19th March, 1988, 15,000 Christians (including myself) converged on the NEC for what was billed as a Day of Prayer for Revival. Many of us were surprised to find that prayer can very effectively be sung, as the vast gathering first learned and then performed Graham Kendrick's second presentation for marching, praise, intercession and declaration, 'Make Way – Shine, Jesus, Shine'. Addressing those present, Bob Dunnett said that he believed God's strategy for the nation now was a Jericho strategy. While also stressing the importance of repentance and humbling ourselves before God, he stated his belief that the powers of darkness would be defeated and the victory won by a declaration of praise and a shout to God. The high note of praise had the power of a spiritual sword. As Christians declared that the powers of darkness must bow down, there would be a breaking and a loosening, a conviction of sin, and a clearing away of evil bondage so that people would believe.

These developments in Birmingham have coincided with similar moves in many other places. Make Way marches have been taking place all over the country ever since it was published in 1986. Most notably, there have been two mighty marches in London organised by a group called 'March for Jesus' which includes Ichthus Christian Fellowship, Pioneer Team and Youth with a Mission. The first was in May 1987, when 15,000 Christians converged on the City, the commercial and banking centre of the nation. During the march, declarations were made against the dishonest practices rampant in the City, and prayer was made that they would be brought to light. Many found it extremely significant that the revelations about the Guiness scandal and insider trading followed soon afterwards. Then came the stockmarket crash in October, which shook the confidence of the entire financial world. The second march, which took place in May 1988, and involved some 55,000 Christians, passed by Parliament, Downing Street, Whitehall and Buckingham Palace, centres of government, as well as the headquarters of several multinational companies.

Make Way is clearly an act of public Christian witness, an engagement in spiritual warfare, and, many would believe, part of God's strategy for revival. It is also an expression of unity between the various churches taking part, and it gives high visibility to the Church in any area where it takes place. It is striking how since 1986 these marches, both large and small, have become a focus for unity up and down the country.

Exciting developments are taking place. Graham Kendrick's presentation, 'Make Way for Christmas' (1988), has been used to great effect in shopping centres and street marches to highlight the real meaning of Christmas in the midst of the largely pagan preparations for the festival. A gathering of some 4,000 church leaders at the NEC has repented of disunity and interceded for the nation at a meeting which lasted several hours. Large-scale marches to witness, pray and proclaim the lordship of Jesus are being held simultaneously in around fifty major centres.

Are these things the stirrings of revival? Only time will tell. At all events, they certainly seem to imply the necessity for unity. For many, following the lead given by such people as Clifford Hill, the key to revival will be to come together in intercession and repentance. For others, there will be the need to make public proclamation of their faith on the streets. I believe that it is a case, not of either/or but of both/and. Provided that everything is done prayerfully and humbly, God will honour and bless his church for being faithful both publicly and privately. But he alone knows if – and if so, when, where and how – he will bring revival. I can only report that the spiritual temperature seems to be rising.

Chapter 13

Prepared for the Best

We must never lose sight of that vision of a future unity, perfect and mature, expressed by Paul in Ephesians chapter 4, verses 7 to 16. I believe firmly that there is among Christians in this country a deep desire for it, and I have tried in this book to point to some ways of turning that longing into reality. In conclusion, I want to look forward to what the Church in England could become, and to summarise some basic steps towards true, as opposed to merely organisational, unity of believers.

First, we must *stop thinking denominationally*. I do not by this mean that we shouldn't value and enjoy the traditions of our particular denomination, but rather that we should sit lightly to them. This applies just as much to members of so-called 'non-denominational' churches, independent fellowships, and House Churches as it does to the 'historic' churches, for we all develop our particular traditions, styles and even vocabulary! Being *Christian* should be more important to us than anything else. We should appreciate other believers as brothers and sisters in Christ, and not tie labels round their necks.

Sometimes we are surprised by situations where denominations simply cease to matter. Last August, I was on holiday with the family in Cornwall. We stayed in a little seaside village with only one church building, a small Anglican church with a normal congregation of less than twelve local residents. It was part of a group ministry led by the large parish church in the neighbouring town. A home group from the town fellowship was given the responsibility of organising a special family service for the holidaymakers staying on the caravan site near the beach. On the Saturday evening, my seven-year-old daughter and I joined the group as they distributed printed invitations around the enormous site. It was a hot, sunny weekend, unusual enough during a typically wet August to tempt most Christians away from church, and I had faith that perhaps one family would turn up for the service. When we arrived at the church on the Sunday morning, however, we found the church nearly full with perhaps sixty adult campers, plus children.

After a very enjoyable, well-prepared yet relaxed service, in which the children had been fully involved, we chatted to other holidaymakers over coffee. None of those I spoke to were from Anglican churches. One couple were Pentecostals from Cardiff, another Free Evangelicals from Sidcup. They had responded to the warmth of the invitation, and had thoroughly enjoyed the service. Even though they were from another tradition, they recognised at once that those leading were committed Christians, that the worship was genuine and the teaching scriptural. Denominational barriers simply didn't divide us.

So on holiday, we had been able to experience a oneness in the Spirit that is more difficult to find in our home towns. In that tiny Cornish village, where we did not have the luxury of choice, we were agreeably surprised by our unity in Christ, and by the quality of what we experienced together.

Back home in our normal living situations, we need to grasp every God-given opportunity of knowing that unity of the Spirit. I have deliberately emphasised that unity starts on a small scale, working upwards from our individual relationship with God, our unity with our marriage partner (if we are married) and within our families, and then with other Christians in our living situation, home group and/or local congregation. But at the same time, we should reach out to other Christians in our neighbourhood across denominational divides. We could make use of an existing structure, like the council of churches, or take a new initiative. It could be that we join a prayer group that is praying for our town. Or we could be part of an inter-church scheme to serve the community in some way. Or we could be involved in a joint church outreach, a Make Way march, or some other evangelistic activity. We could even, like the irrepressible House Church leader Gerald Coates, throw a party and invite a very varied bunch of Christians to it![1]

If we do engage in this sort of project, we are immediately putting into practice the idea of 'the church in the city' (or locality) for which I have been arguing. As city groupings link up nationally, we can express the Gospel very powerfully and publically through our unity. I have looked at some examples of this: the 'Keep Sunday Special' campaign, the support for David Alton's Bill on abortion, and the Make Way marches throughout Britain.

If we do not feel that we have the time or the opportunity to do anything like this in addition to our commitments within our own local church, at least we can start thinking differently. As Paul writes, 'Do not conform any longer to the pattern of this world, but be transformed by the renewing of your mind' (Romans 12.2). Thinking denominationally is, quite simply, a worldly habit, and God wants to re-educate our thought processes. We can also make more of an effort to cross the barriers that undoubtedly exist within our own church, while at the same time becoming more open, humble and friendly towards members of other churches.

We also need to *take the Ephesians chapter 4 ministries more seriously*. We need to heed God's chosen ministers of the hour who happen to come from traditions other than our own. We may not like the fact that God is speaking through an Anglican apostle, a Baptist teacher, a Methodist evangelist, a House Church prophet or a Roman Catholic pastor, but we need to open our eyes, recognise the fact, and learn from these people. We need to pay particular attention to anointed men and women who are fulfilling the apostolic ministry of building unity between churches. The ministries of Ephesians chapter 4 are, after all, given so that the church might reach a mature unity in Christ (v.13). In each city, town and community, I believe that there will increasingly be

191

raised up 'apostles of unity' whom God will use to bring Christians closer together.

We need to recognise men and women exercising a ministry within a locality which can be shared across local church and denominational barriers with no strings attached. There should never be a sense that in order to benefit from so-and-so's ministry we have to join their church or 'come under their authority'. Any true authority that they convey is that of the Word and Spirit of God working through them. Essentially, it is not their ministry but God's.

I also believe that whole fellowships can exercise a specific ministry, and thus give a lead to other churches in a community. In Bristol, for example, one church is outstanding in bringing enquirers to a point of commitment to Christ, and then nurturing the new converts. Another, which has set up an evangelism team, has helped my church develop one of our own. Yet another has been an example to many others in how to give away a large proportion of its income to missionary activity.

We need to beware of thinking that these ministries can only emerge in a particular church or denomination. Leaders tend to be very parochial about who they allow to preach and teach in their churches. For example, this thinking has appeared to be the norm in the House Church movement, and has led to the unfortunate assumption by some of their leaders that God cannot raise up effective ministries from within the historic denominations. Fortunately, this view is changing, and such informal gatherings as the National Charismatic Leaders' Conference (a smallish group that meets by invitation only), national leaders' meetings sponsored by the EA, and similar, locally based meetings like the Bristol Celebration leaders' group, ensure that channels of communication and friendship are kept open. The signs are of deepening trust and mutual appreciation at any rate in most evangelical and charismatic circles.

If the church is to reach a state of unity, we must let spiritually anointed men and women minister. What is the use of God raising them up if they are not allowed to function? At the same time, however, we have to test each ministry to see if it is from God. Is it scriptural? Does it cause the wrong sort of division and disruption (granted that the Holy Spirit will always bring a stubborn response from those who are determined to resist him)? What is the quality of the person's life and behaviour? I know of some people with international ministries who are very awkward to deal with and difficult to have in your home (it is usually a useful acid test to see how a visiting leader copes with your children!). True holiness shows in a person's behaviour. Jesus taught, 'By their *fruit* you will recognise them' (Matt. 7.16) – not by their ministry.

At the same time, we should appreciate the contribution of *every individual and every church* to unity. We have seen in I Corinthians, chapter 12, and Ephesians chapter 4, verse 16, how Paul emphasises that the church can be a healthy body only if *each individual member is functioning properly*. Although the church needs leaders with the ministry gifts of Ephesians, chapter 4, verse 11, to fulfil God's purpose, it equally needs the participation of every Christian. Leaders cannot afford to be superior about less obviously gifted members of the church. I remember hearing a House Church leader refer casually to 'the rank and file', and reflecting wryly that the wheel had come full circle from a commitment to the priesthood of all believers to a full-blown clergy/laity division. There is a danger that fellowships with many full-time workers, high-powered evangelism teams, and so on will cause the vast majority of members in secular employment to think that they are second-class Christians. On the contrary, full-time workers have the role of enablers and equippers, catalysts for the whole church to get on the move.

As far as *churches* are concerned, we must remember that the model for unity in the Scriptures is never that of uniformity. God himself is gloriously diverse as Father, Son and Holy Spirit. So we should not expect the unity we seek to be monochrome. No one church or denomination has the right to expect unity to come because all the other churches finally join it and become like it. The Inter-Church Process has accepted this principle on a national level, and it should be thoroughly endorsed at the local level as well, particularly by the House Churches. We should accept that God is working in traditions other than our own to bring renewal and revival to his whole Church, and respect the unique gift and blessing that each local church brings to the whole body of Christ in a locality.

If we are all to make our contribution to the building up of the Church in unity, *our relationships with other Christians must be truthful and loving.* We must be prepared to 'speak the truth in love' (Eph 4.15) – and to live it out in love. 'Truth' refers first and foremost to *doctrinal truth.* God is a God of truth, and his Word, the Bible, is the basis of doctrinal truth and the yardstick of Christian behaviour. As the Articles of Religion of the Church of England state, 'Holy Scripture containeth all things necessary to salvation' (Article 6). We need to know it through and through, and to use it to check out any teaching that we hear, as the Berean Jews did in Acts chapter 17, verse 11. False teaching has been present at every stage of church history, and is more that ever apparent now. Many Christians run after new fads, and it sometimes seems that the more dogmatic and one-sided a preacher is, the more what he says will be swallowed by a gullible audience that has not bothered to apply scriptural tests to the message that is being preached.

We live with a legacy of centuries of denominational theology based on traditional and time-honoured interpretations of Scripture, some of which clearly have no scriptural foundation whatsoever. In addition to this, the long-suffering Christian public in the West have recently been treated to overemphases and distortions such as 'prosperity teaching' and an attitude to healing that turns faith into a strong 'believism' which the Christian has to work up in himself. We have been asked to swallow rigidly structured 'shepherding', and various pseudo-political versions of the kingdom of God, both of the right and the left. Some of this teaching is partially biblically-based, but fails to look at the verses that do not agree with it, while some has only the slenderest possible foundation. We need to withstand false teaching lovingly but firmly, while distinguishing between the essential truths that unite us (e.g. the Incarnation and Atoning Death of Christ, his bodily Resurrection and Ascension, the coming of the Holy Spirit and his work in the believer, and the Second Coming of Christ), and secondary matters. If there is disagreement on the vital issues, there should be no need for a debate, whereas on other questions like infant baptism, gifts of the spirit and the Rapture there should be loving and continuing discussion between born-again brothers and sisters who hold differing views.

God is calling us to a heart-unity that actually transcends these issues, though it does not remove them. It is vital that any discussion of doctrine is done in love, with a respect for the person we disagree with, if not necessarily for their views. Let's accept the fact of our doctrinal diversity, provided that we are united on essentials. Richard Baxter's much-quoted dictum can be slipped in at this point: 'In things essential, unity; in things doubtful, liberty; in all things, charity.'

Living and speaking the truth with Christian brothers and sisters does not refer simply to doctrine. The Bible is also the yardstick of a Christian's *behaviour*. This is expressed in I John as 'walking in the light': 'if we walk in the light, as he is in the light, we have fellowship with one another, and the blood of Jesus, his Son, purifies us from all sin (I John 1.7). Paul calls it 'living by the Spirit' (Gal. 5.16), and the Spirit does not contradict the Bible, but rather bears it out and enables us to live according to its teaching. Ephesians chapter 4 goes on from verse 17 with a long section, continuing up to chapter 6, verse 9, on how to live the Christian life and relate to people in the right way. Interestingly, Paul uses the same picture as John to describe this: 'Live as children of light . . . and find out what pleases the Lord'(5.8–9).

Basically, we English Christians are very bad at being open with one another in love; in fact, very bad at respecting and loving one another at all. This has been noted and commented upon recently, e.g. by Clifford Hill and Robert Amess. For this we simply need to repent and do better. We have to start at the personal and local level, in our marriages (how repressed and uncommunicative we do seem to be – is it a national trait?), and in our local church, where petty hurt and jealousy can be allowed to fester for years. Leaders need training in how to speak the truth in love (there are books on the subject),[2] so that they can do it, and teach their people how to. Whole congregations need to be cleansed and experience the love and forgiveness of Christ releasing them from sin.

Once we have recognised and begun to tackle the problem in ourselves and our own church, it becomes much easier to face the problem that exists between Christians in different churches. Perhaps this problem is more acutely seen among leaders than anyone. As a leader, I am very aware of this. We tend to be suspicious of one another, defensive, proud or ashamed of our own set-up, and probably with a great deal of underlying insecurity which leads us either to dominate or to resent. We can criticise each other blatantly and unashamedly behind each other's backs. Praise God that some of this is changing! In Bristol, for example, we are beginning to experience a greater warmth of friendship within the Celebration group – and beyond it. But we have a great deal further to go before we establish real trust and openness between us, and a genuine sense that we are all working in complete harmony. Probably only a major new visitation of the Holy Spirit in revival power will be able to achieve such a breakthrough among us.

Truth for the Christian always goes hand-in-hand with love. John Stott puts it very well in his commentary on Ephesians: 'Truth becomes hard if it is not softened by love; love becomes soft if it is not strengthened by truth.'[3] It is absolutely no use insisting on doctrinal purity or confronting a brother about some fault if this is not done in love. The Anglican vicar Tony Higton is a good example of a Christian who is prepared to take a public and costly stand about doctrinal and moral errors in the church (in his case, the Church of England) and yet do so in a loving, non-vindictive way. We need to examine our own hearts carefully before truth-telling, and ask ourselves what our real motives are, whether we have forgiven others for past hurts, and whether we really do 'follow the way of love' (I Cor. 14.1).

We need to remember that *Jesus is coming back for a perfect bride*. Paul tells us that it is Christ's purpose to present the church to himself as 'a radiant church, without stain or wrinkle or any other blemish, but holy and blameless' (Eph. 5.27). Jesus is coming back, and he is coming for a church which, as far as possible, has prepared herself (Rev. 19.7).[4] We have a responsibility in this. Jesus himself taught the importance of being prepared for the bridegroom's return in the parable of the Ten Virgins (Matt. 25.1–3), and in the parable of the servants who had to be awake and ready for their master's arrival (Luke 12.35–40). The Bible teaches how we should do this, by ensuring that our lives match up to God's standards: 'You ought to live holy and godly lives as you look forward to the day of God and speed its coming. . . . So then, dear friends, since you are looking forward to this, make every effort to be found spotless, blameless and at peace with him' (II Peter 3.11, 12, 14).

Part of our perfection is to be a united church. The words 'mature' and 'perfect' are translations of the same Greek word. Ephesians, chapter 4, verse 13, speaks of our future 'unity in the faith and in the knowledge of the Son of God' as being a sign – perhaps the main sign – of our maturity. It will equally be a sign of our perfection. Disunity represents a major blemish marring the beauty of the bride of Christ, and I do not believe that the Lord will return until we have reached that complete unity that alone is acceptable to him. Stott writes, 'Just as unity needs to be maintained *visibly*, so it needs to be attained fully'.[5] In order for that to happen, we need to make an effort. Do we want the Lord to return in our generation?

If so, we will be praying and working towards, among other things, the unity of his church, for he will not return for a bribe who is less than perfect.

As we begin to catch the vision for this, it will be a great help if we recognise that *we stand together against a common enemy*. It is amazing how a shared enemy can draw together the most unlikely allies. It took a Hitler to unite the capitalist USA with the communist Soviet Union. We Christians are already brothers in the family of God, and yet having Satan as an enemy doesn't unite us. How blind and foolish we are! The victory has already been won on Calvary; we simply have to declare it, and stand up to the forces of a foe who has been rendered powerless. We have all the advantages, if only we would realise that we are in a spiritual war, and then unite and fight shoulder to shoulder. As long as the enemy is fighting a disunited church, he can win many skirmishes, because he can sit back while we fight one another, and pick off the spiritual stragglers.

The very existence of the devil is denied in many denominational theological colleges where ministers are trained. This was my own experience, and so I was launched on an Anglican parish quite unprepared to deal with some of the problems that presented themselves. As a result, my training in spiritual warfare took place on the job – not a bad thing, perhaps, but I would have welcomed some systematic preparation beforehand. We must all learn to recognise and resist Satan. Leaders urgently need to teach about this. All Christians need to learn how to discern the devil's presence and his tricks (an important aspect of the gift of discernment), how to resist temptation, how to cast out evil spirits, how to pray against the forces of darkness, and how to confront, graciously but uncompromisingly, people who are being manipulated by Satan to inflict evil and injustice on others. We also need to understand what our spiritual weapons are, and how to use them (Eph. 6.10–18).

The strongest sense I have so far ever had of being part of God's mighty army in the spiritual battle was at the Day

of Prayer for Revival at the National Exhibition Centre
in Birmingham in March 1988. There must have been
Christians there from every conceivable denomination
and 'stream', but as the 11,000 of us filled that great
hall, we simply knew that we were 'all one in Christ
Jesus' (Gal. 3.28). Singing in unison the Lord's words
to Graham Kendrick's setting, we felt the powers of
darkness in our nation beginning to tremble:

> *I will build my church*
> *And the gates of hell*
> *Shall not prevail against it.*
> *So you powers in the heavens above, bow down!*
> *And you powers on the earth below, bow down!*
> *And acknowledge that Jesus is Lord.*[6]

It is tremendously helpful to be together in the same
place worshipping and praying if we are to know unity in
spiritual warfare. But we must also remember that God's
army is always united in spirit, even when we are alone
and physically apart, and that God, the master strategist,
can win battles with a 'Gideon's army' of scattered and
solitary Christians if they are dedicated and united in
prayer.

But it is no use our working and praying for unity for
its own sake or even for the sake of the church. *Our unity
must be outward-looking.* It exists ultimately for the sake of
the world. Jesus prayed that we might all be one so that
the world might believe that the Father had sent his Son,
and loved them as much as he loved him (John 17.21,
23). So there is a tremendous evangelistic thrust to our
unity.

Certainly, our nation needs the gospel as never before
in this century. Of the UK's adult population, 85 per
cent do not go to church regularly (90 per cent in
England), and young people are appallingly ignorant
of the Bible, the teaching of Jesus, and what it means
to be a Christian. At the same time, society is being
increasingly shaken by forces of disorder and lawlessness
over which we have very little control. Although secular

199

sociologists would not accept it, Christians must admit that the responsibility for this state of affairs rests largely on our shoulders. We cannot make society perfect, but, as Jesus taught in the Sermon on the Mount (Matt. 5.13–16), we certainly can and should act as salt (a preservative, keeping society from decaying) and light (showing people clearly what the gospel is and how they can know and follow Christ).

If Christians begin to unite, and are open about their unity, the British public will definitely begin to sit up and take notice. I believe that there are a vast number of people searching for a meaning to life and for some certainties in the midst of the shifting sand of contemporary standards and ideals, who would respond to the gospel if only it were presented to them by a strong church speaking with a united voice. We should be seen as united not simply in our negative reactions to blasphemous films, unjust legislation, pornography on TV, or whatever – however correct such reactions undoubtedly are. We need to be offering a *positive alternative* to all sections of our society: the message of salvation in its deepest and broadest aspects. *We should unite at the highest and most biblical level possible of Christian life and witness.*

In Chapter 3, I looked at the first church in Jerusalem, and suggested that it provides us with an outstanding model of what church life can be. We should not copy it slavishly – how could we, 2,000 years later! – but we should check that all the elements that they experienced are present in our church life. We should seek to be united in *the power of the Holy Spirit*. This means, in my personal view, an acceptance of the supernatural gifts of the Holy Spirit as valid and operational today. It means that our evangelism will include healings, the casting out of demons, and other miraculous signs.

We should also want to be be united in *the love and fellowship of the Holy Spirit*, sharing our lives at the deepest level. We must not be content with superficiality in our relationships, but teach and practice commitment to God, one another, and the church of which we are members. We should be prepared to be accountable, not just to leaders, but to the whole body of Christ, by being really open about our feelings, needs, visions, plans and, if necessary, hurts and sins (in order to receive healing and forgiveness). We should be willing to give generously to God's work, and to share our homes and possessions with one another as far as we are able.

By stating these ideals as something that we can realistically aim for in our search for unity, I do mean to say that we can't unite at a less ambitious level. Certainly, we can. For example, it is perfectly possible for charismatic evangelicals, who accept the use of the I Corinthians chapter 12 gifts, to be involved in a mission with non-charismatic evangelicals, who do not. It is simply that the level of unity achieved will not be as deep or as powerful. We will be falling short of God's very best, because I believe that he wants us all to be using those gifts to make our evangelism much more effective.

Such a depth of unity can probably only come about through a *large-scale revival*. I believe that England is ripe for revival. In 1988 we celebrated the 250th anniversary of the conversion of John Wesley, which led to the eighteenth century Methodist Revival. We desperately need the fire of God to fall upon the church in England in an even more fundamental and widespread way than at that time. The main enemies of the gospel in our nation at the moment are probably affluence and apathy, coupled with a ruthless 'Yuppie' drive to make it to the top. In our society, successful people do not think they need God, and ambitious achievers regard the need for God as a fatal sign of weakness. On the other hand, the poor and disadvantaged are so distanced from the largely middle-class churches that they don't believe Christians have anything to offer them.

The only way to a spiritual breakthrough in this situation is by tried and tested methods: prayer, prayer and more prayer, springing from a deep desire to see God glorified, coupled with sincere repentance, and a willingness to stand up and be counted as Christians.

I personally agree with Bob Dunnett and Graham Kendrick that the church needs to use praise and prayer on the streets both as a spiritual weapon and as a perfectly valid means of Christians becoming visible in all their united strength. If events like the Marches for Jesus are backed by concerted prayer, and used in the providence of God (who, we must always remember, cannot be manipulated by our prayers), they can be a very powerful witness indeed. I am reminded of the Pentecostal preacher Jean Darnall's vision (of over twenty years ago) of fire sweeping down from John O' Groats to Land's End.[7] We need the fire of God to do just that.

However, as I made clear earlier, revival does not of itself guarantee unity. We can have a revival in our church or denomination and yet not be bonded heart to heart with our brothers and sisters down the road. Yet if our wills are set in the right direction, revival will move us much further on. As one writer has put it, 'Where the Spirit of God has full control sectarian barriers disappear, as the dry patches that divide pool from pool on the shore are swamped by the rising tide.'[8]

On holiday in Cornwall, we have often watched as the little rock pools, each with its crab or starfish or collection of anemones, are quite suddenly flooded by the crashing waves of the incoming tide. Swimming in the sea is much more alarming than swimming in a rock pool – but it's much more exhilarating. We need the mighty Spirit of God to come crashing into our pools (some tiny, some actually quite imposing and full of rather important-looking apostolic fish) and lift us over the edge into the limitless ocean, where we can all swim freely together.

When this happens, we need to be spiritually on the alert. Such a depth of unity is sure to provoke a hostile reaction – but this in turn will lead to even deeper unity. Along with great blessing, the Jerusalem church experienced considerable persecution. In particular, it was the religious authorities who objected to what the followers of Jesus were doing. They did not like their public proclamation of Jesus as the Messiah, or the healing miracles that they were performing. Basically, they did not like the fact that the Christians were so successful spiritually: we read that they were filled with jealousy (Acts 5.17). As a result, the new believers were arrested, flogged, stoned and beheaded. Acts chapter 8, verses 1 to 3, tells of the great persecution which broke out in Jerusalem and resulted in all the Christians except the apostles being scattered throughout Judea and Samaria.

In a theocracy like Israel, the religious authorities were also the secular authorities. In such a society, Christians will always be persecuted unless the state is genuinely Christianised. We can see this in our own times from the persecution that Christians are undergoing in a Hindu state like Nepal, an Islamic state like Iran, and a Communist state like Romania (communism being clearly a creed, though an atheistic one). Great Britain is nominally Christian; England is by far the least Christian part of it, according to the churchgoing statistics. Christians here do not suffer outright persecution. The greatest threat of that so far has been the decision of a few ultra-left-wing local authorities to withdraw police protection from those who oppose their policy of positive discrimination in favour of homosexuals.

But there are more subtle forms of persecution. There is, for example, the disdain of those who would dismiss any Christians who take what the Bible teaches literally as naïve and fanatical fundamentalists. Such people would happily echo the then Bishop of Bristol's words to John Wesley: 'Sir, the pretending to extraordinary revelations and gifts of the Holy Ghost is a horrid thing – a very horrid thing.'[9] Although there are members of the religious establishment in this country who are sympathetic to a more conservative theology, to evangelicalism, and even to the charismatic movement within their denominations, many church leaders take a more cautious, even disapproving line. For them, Christian unity is simply a matter of denominations working together in a friendly fashion, while accepting an agreed liberal interpretation of Scripture almost entirely shorn of its supernatural dimension, along with a liberal or mildly socialist programme of political action (I write as a political liberal/democrat who does not necessarily accept the party line). It does not involve joining together to pray, worship and work for the conversion of England and the renewing of our society, which is surely what Christians in England are being challenged to do by God.

I believe that as the movement towards authentic unity gains momentum, it will involve all committed believers, as well as many disillusioned church people, including leaders, who are searching for spiritual reality. Others, however, are likely to react in an angry and hostile manner. A deep division, cutting across all the denominations, will become apparent between those Christians who are really serious about their faith and determined to follow and proclaim the God of the Bible in the power of the Spirit,[10] and those who are in the business of perpetuating religious institutions and propagating false theology.

In this situation, the non-Christian British public will be attracted to the true life of God in the true people of God. We read of Jesus that ordinary people loved to listen to him (Mark 12.37). The Jerusalem church enjoyed the favour of all the people because they could see the love and power of God so clearly in the way the Christians lived (Acts 2.47). When British Christians are fully committed to God, filled with his Spirit, united heart-to-heart, proclaiming the gospel publicly, and being seen to care for the needy, amazingly large numbers of people will be converted. In every city, town and village we shall see the phenomenon of Jerusalem: 'The Lord added to their number daily those who were being saved' (Acts 2.47). Hostility to this will only cause the unity to deepen.

I see Christians in England, and in the UK as a whole, poised on the verge of what could be a crucial step forward into the powerful purposes of God. He desires his church to be united, and this could be achieved here in our generation. But for this to happen, there has to be repentance for past and present disunity, a humble desire to do better, the will to persevere in joint prayer, worship, Jesus Action and evangelism, a willingness to stand up and be counted, more faith that revival can happen in our land, and the determination to be satisfied with nothing less than God's best. The measure of that is the Bible; the means of achieving it is the Holy Spirit, who has been given to be with us for ever. We need to be more and more open and obedient to him. The times are crucial; it is up to us. 'He who has an ear, let him hear what the Spirit says to the churches' (Rev. 2.11).

If we are obedient, the words of the familiar song will stop sounding like a tired relic of the 1970s and begin to resound with the reality of God in action now:

> *For I'm building a people of power*
> *And I'm making a people of praise,*
> *Who will move through this land by My Spirit,*
> *And will glorify My precious Name.*
> *Build your church, Lord*
> *Make us strong, Lord,*
> *Join our hearts, Lord through your Son*
> *Make us one, Lord, in Your Body,*
> *In the Kingdom of Your Son.*[11]

© Dave Richards/Thankyou Music

Notes

Chapter 1

1 From Graham Kendrick, 'Make Way', Copyright © 1986 Make Way Music. Administered by Thankyou Music, P.o.Box 75, Eastbourne, E. Sussex BN23 6NW, UK used by permission. Thank You

2 This name is given to the movement that has introduced Pentecostal theology and practice (e.g. 'speaking in tongues') into the historic denominations.

3 For careful definitions and analyses of these words and their use, see article in the *Theological Dictionary of the New Testament*, ed. Colin Brown (Paternoster, 1975–78): 'Heart', by T. Sorg (vol. 2, pp.180–184); 'Soul', by G. Harder (vol. 3, pp. 679–688).

4 Ibid. art. on 'mind' by J. Goetzmann, (vol. 2, pp. 616–20).

5 Ibid. art. on 'reason, mind, understanding – "nous"', by G. Harder, vol. 3, pp. 122–130.

6 In *'Enemy Territory – the Christian Struggle for the Modern World* (Hodder & Stoughton, 1987), pp. 191–2, Andrew Walker argues strongly for the use of 'modernist' as opposed to 'liberal'. I have preferred 'liberal' as being the more popular and easily identifiable label – though all labels are liable to be inaccurate and should be used with caution!

Chapter 2

1 Brother Andrew, *God's Smuggler* (Hodder & Stoughton, 1967).

2 *Renewal* first appeared in January 1966. Its first editor, Michael Harper, concluded his introductory editorial, 'We hope *Renewal* will play its part in this vital rediscovery by the Church of the power of the Holy Spirit.' *Renewal* has been in the forefront of this

rediscovery since then. It is now edited by Edward England.

3 David du Plessis, *The Spirit Bade Me Go* (pub. D. du Plessis, 1961).

4 The Rev Canon Michael Harper is a prolific author and a leader of Charismatic Renewal (particularly in the Anglican Communion). He was the original editor of *Renewal* magazine.

5 The Rev Colin Urquhart, an Anglican minister with an international teaching and healing ministry, now leads the interdenominational Bethany Fellowship based in Sussex.

Chapter 3

1 See R.V.G. Tasker, *St John* (Tyndale N T Commentaries, IVP, 1960), p. 70.

2 e.g. Colin Urquhart, as he describes in his book *When the Spirit comes* (Hodder & Stoughton, 1974), ch. 2.

3 Gordon MacDonald, *Ordering Your Private World* (Highland Books, 1985), pp. 91–3.

4 John Stott, *God's New Society* (IVP, 1979), p. 110.

Chapter 4

1 J.B. Phillips, *The Young Church in Action* (Collins, 1955), p. 11.

2 David Coffey brings out the importance of the supernatural dimension of the faith in *Build That Bridge* (Kingsway, 1986), pp. 144–5.

3 For example, the evangelical Sanford D. Hull has isolated 22 exegetical difficulties in I Corinthians chapter 11, verses 2–16, the passage on head-covering, in *Equal To Serve*, by Gretchen Gaebelein Hull (Fleming H. Revell, 1987), Appendix II, pp. 252–7.

4 I.H. Marshall *The Acts of the Apostles*, (Tyndale N T Commentaries, IVP, 1980), p. 83.

5 The subject of 'the Church in the House' is very fully dealt with by David Lillie in his book *Beyond Charisma* (Paternoster, 1981), chapter 7.

6 'Acts 86' was a conference on Charismatic Renewal with participation from Christians from most Western European, and some Eastern bloc, countries.

Chapter 5

1 We may compare the fact that although through his death, Jesus has won for us the forgiveness of our sins, we still have to enter into the reality of this, not simply by our initial repentance and faith, which justifies us (Acts 2.38), but also by our ongoing confession of sin and receiving forgiveness, through which we are sanctified (Matt. 5.12, James 5.16).
2 C.O. Buchanan, E.L. Mascall, J.I. Packer, G.D. Leonard, *Growing into Union* (S P C K, 1970).
3 Joyce Huggett, *Conflict; Friend or Foe?* (Kingsway, 1984), pp. 35–43.

Chapter 6

1 J. Jeremias, *The Central Message of the New Testament* (S C M Press, 1965), p. 17.
2 E.g. I.H. Marshall, *The Gospel of Luke* (Paternoster, 1978), p. 592.
3 *Dictionary of New Testament Theology*, art. 'Fellowship' by J. Schattenmann, vol. 1, p. 642.
4 Michael Harper, *A New Way of Living* (Hodder & Stoughton, 1973).
5 E.g. in particular, besides M. Harper's book, the gripping account by Graham Pulkingham, the rector of the church, in *Gathered for Power* (Hodder & Stoughton, 1972).

Chapter 7

1 For much of what follows, I am indebted to the succinct yet scholarly articles of *The History of Christianity* (Lion, 1977), ed. T. Dowley.
2 Ibid., art. 'Reform', by James Atkinson, p. 386.
3 Ibid., art. 'The Pentecostals', by James Dunn, p. 618.
4 David Watson quotes himself, and comments, in

his autobiography, *You Are My God* (Hodder & Stoughton, 1983), p. 102.

5 For a comprehensive history and subtle analysis of the House-Church Movement, see Andrew Walker, *Restoring the Kingdom* (Hodder & Stoughton, 1985).

6 David Coffey (op. cit., p. 17) comments, 'I am concerned that church leaders at national level who have a common concern for the Gospel should recognise the body of Christ in its fullest expression, and be ready to engage in bridge-building dialogue.' I would want to extend that concern to leaders at *local level*, and indeed to every member of the body of Christ.

7 David Watson, *I believe in the Church* (Hodder, 1978), p. 355.

8 Lion *History of Christianity*, art. 'Organising for Unity', by Colin Buchanan, p. 634.

9 Ibid., p. 636.

Chapter 8

1 These statements are based on statistics quoted in the *UK Christian Handbook*, 1989/90 Edition, ed. P. Brierley (Marc Europe/EA/Bible Soc. 1988), especially. p. 150.

2 Quoted in the Preface of *Views from the Pews* (BCC and Catholic Truth Society, 1986).

3 *Reflections*, and *Observations* were also published in 1986 by the BCC and the CTS.

4 The details of the Swanwick conference reported below, including the text of the Swanwick Declaration, are taken from *Vision One*, the magazine of the BCC, Jan. 1988, no. 69.

5 The full proposals, together with a summary of the work done during the Inter – Church Process, are contained in *Churches Together in Pilgrimage* (BCC/CTS, 1989).

6 Clive Calver, *He Brings Us Together* (Hodder & Stoughton, 1987).

7 Martin Wroe, art. 'The evangelicals marching as to

war', in the *Independent*, 20th April, 1988.

8 Colin Blakely, art. 'Alton's Crusade' in *Leadership Today*, August 1988, p. 25.

9 The EA is responding to the Inter – Church Process with caution – see David Lee art . 'Strangers and Pilgrims' in *Leadership Today*, April 1989, p.18.

Chapter 9

1 George Carey, *The Meeting of the Waters* (Hodder & Stoughton, 1985), pp. 50–59.

2 Watson, 'You are My God', p. 99. Michael Harper puts his point of view in *This is the Day* (Hodder, 1979), which also contains some important joint statements and reports.

3 Robert Amess, *One in the Truth* (Kingsway, 1988), p. 98.

4 R. Bultmann, *History of the New Testament*, vol.1 (Eng. trans. S C M Press, 1952), p. 45.

5 J. Hick (ed.), *The Myth of God Incarnate* (S C M. Press, 1977)

6 Du Plessis, op. cit., pp. 13–14.

7 David L. Edwards and John Stott, *Essentials* (Hodder, 1988).

8 Clifford Hill, *The Evangelical Scandal* (Decade of Evangelism, 1980), pp. 3–4.

9 Nick Page, art. 'Cutting Edge' in *Leadership Today'*, May 1988.

10 Amess, op. cit., pp. 12 & 13.

11 On bridging the white/black-led church divide, see Philip Mohabir's exciting and moving book, *Building Bridges* (Hodder & Stoughton, 1988), especially the final chapter, 'Closing the gap' pp. 197–208.

12 The term 'Third Wave' was coined by the American missiologist and church-growth expert C. Peter Wagner. He writes, 'The Third Wave began around 1980 with the opening of an increasing number of traditional evangelical churches and institutions to the supernatural working of the Holy Spirit, even though they were not, nor did they wish to become,

either Pentecostal or Charismatic.' (*Christian Life* magazine, January 1966 – quoted by John Wimber in the Introduction to *Riding the Third Wave*, ed. Kevin Springer, Marshall Pickering, 1987 , p. 31).

13 T.A. Smail (ed.), *Gospel and Spirit: a Joint Statement* (Fountain Trust, 1977), pp. 5 and 9. This text is also Appendix B of Michael Harper, *This is the Day*.

14 Donald Bridge and David Phypers, *Spiritual gifts and the church* (I.V.P., 1973), pp. 29 and 31.

15 John Noble, *House Churches: Will They Survive?* (Kingsway, 1988), p. 16.

Chapter 10

1 For my view on the vital role for Christian unity of the church in the locality, I am indebted particularly to the thinking of David Lillie in *Beyond Charisma*, especially chapters 5 and 6, pp. 38–58.

2 Jimmy and Carol Owens, *Come Together* (Lexicon Music, 1972).

3 Lillie, op. cit., p. 45.

Chapter 11

1 This exegesis of Matthew, chapter 24, verse 14, is not universally accepted. R.T. France, to my mind unconvincingly, argues that verses 4 to 35 form a continuous whole referring to the coming judgment of Jerusalem, and not at all to the Second Coming (France, *The Gospel According to St Matthew*, I V P, 1985, pp. 333–347). Not all theologians of mission accept it either, e.g. Samuel Escobar, art. 'The Return of Christ', in *The New Face of Evangelicalism*, ed. C. Rene Padilla (Hodder & Stoughton, 1976) p. 262. My interpretation betrays my 'classical pre-millenialist' leanings (not dispensationalist), and the influence of the theology of Roger Forster! It is still, however, accepted by many commentators, and by the Lausanne Covenant (drafted at the International Congress on World Evangelisation at Lausanne in 1974), which states, 'The promise of his (Jesus')

coming is a further spur to our evangelism, for we remember his word that the Gospel must first be preached to all nations' – see J. Stott, *The Lausanne Covenant, an Exposition and Commentary'* (World Wide Publications, 1975), pp. 56–61.

Chapter 12

1 For another look at church-decision making 'in the Spirit', see Floyd McClung, *Father, Make Us One* (Kingsway, 1987), ch. 8, pp. 89–100.
2 Michael Green, *I believe in Satan's Downfall* (Hodder & Stoughton, 1981), p. 251.
3 Jimmy and Carol Owens, *If my people* (Lexicon Music, 1974).
4 Brian Mills, in art. 'Call to Repentance' in *Prophecy Today*, vol. 4 no. 2, March/April 1988, p. 9.
5 An outstanding example is the Battle of Britain. The battle began on 8th August, 1941. Hitler planned to invade England on 14th September. King George VI called a National Day of Prayer on 7th September. By the end of Sunday, 15th September, the tide of the enemy offensive had been turned. These events are reported, with many other examples of answers to prayer during the Second World War, in *The Trumpet Sounds for Britain*, by David E. Gardner (Christian Foundation Publications, 1981) – see in particular chapter 6.
6 Quoted by Colin Whittaker in *Great Revivals* (Marshalls, 1984), p. 86.
7 'Call to Repentance', p. 7.

Chapter 13

1 See Gerald Coates, art. 'Why Build Bridges?', *Pioneer Bulletin*, Autumn 1988, p. 11.
2 e.g. William Backus, *Telling Each Other the Truth* (Bethany House), and McClung, op. cit., ch. 4 'Rules for Relationships' and ch. 7 on confronting leaders.
3 Stott, op. cit., p. 172.
4 Not everyone agrees with this interpretation, which

again betrays my premillenialist stance. For a well-stated version of the opposite position, see Michael Harper, *That we may be one* (Hodder & Stoughton, 1983) ch. 13. However, I am relieved to note that my views seem to be in line with those of John Stott, who writes (*God's New Society*, p. 228), 'The "sanctification" appears to refer to the present process of making her (the bride) holy in character and conduct by the power of the indwelling spirit.'

5 Ibid., p 169. *I wll build my church*. Copyright © 1988 Make Way Music. Administered in Europe by Thankyou Music, P.o. Box 75, Eastbourne, E. Sussex BN 23 6NW, UK. Used by permission.

6 Graham Kendrick, *Make Way Handbook* (Kingsway, 1988), pp. 66–67.

7 Jean Darnall, *Heaven, Here I Come* (Lakeland, 1974), p. 112.

8 Quoted in Amess, op. cit., p. 155.

9 Quoted in G.R. Cragg, *The Church and the Age of Reason, 1648–1789* (Penguin, 1960), p. 150.

10 E.g. conservative theologians of all denominations are beginning to come together and speak out against the onslaughts of liberal/modernist theology. In *Different Gospels*, ed. Andrew Walker (Hodder & Stoughton 1988), a wide variety of theologians and church leaders, Roman Catholic, Orthodox and Protestant, defend the central truths of Christianity and offer their critiques of modernism. The C.S. Lewis Study Centre, founded and directed by Walker, which sponsored this publication, has the aim of analysing the relationship between religion and modernity, combating modernism, and intelligently presenting an orthodox position. Walker ends his introduction with the stirring words, 'We who have heard and responded to the gospel of hope are marching to Zion' (p. 20).

11 Dave Richards, 'For I'm building a people of power', Copyright © 1977 Thankyou Music P.O. Box 75 Eastbourne, E. Sussex, UK. BN 23 6NW used by permission.

Amess, Robert, *One in the Truth* (Kingsway, 1988).

BBC and CTS (pub.) *Churches Together in Pilgrimage,* 1989

BBC and CTS (pub.) *Observations,* 1986.

BBC and CTS (pub.) *Reflections,* 1986.

BBC and CTS (pub.) *Views from the Pews,* 1986

Bridge, Donald and Phypers, David, *Spiritual gifts and the church* (IVP, 1973).

Brown, Colin (ed.), *Theological Dictionary of the New Testament* (Paternoster, 1975-78).

Calver, Clive, *He Brings Us Together* (Hodder & Stoughton, 1987)

Carey, George, *The Meeting of the Waters* (Hodder & Stoughton, 1985).

Coffey, David, *Build That Bridge* (Kingsway, 1986).

Dowley, Tim (ed.), *The History of Christianity* (Lion, 1977).

du Plessis, David, *The Spirit Bade Me Go* (pub. D. du Plessis, 1961).

Edwards, David, and Stott, John, *Essentials* (Hodder, 1988).

Green, Michael, *I believe in Satan's Downfall* (Hodder & Stoughton, 1981).

Harper, Michael, *A New Way of Living* (Hodder & Stoughton, 1973).

Harper, Michael, *That we may be one* (Hodder & Stoughton, 1983).

Harper, Michael, *This Is The Day* (Hodder & Stoughton, 1979).

Huggett, Joyce, *Conflict: Friend or Foe?* (Kingsway, 1984).

Jeremias, Joachim, *The Central Message of the New Testament* (SCM Press, 1965)

Lillie, David, *Beyond Charisma* (Paternoster, 1981).

McClung, Floyd, *Father, Make Us One* (Kingsway, 1987).

MacDonald, Gordon, *Ordering Your Private World* (Highland Books, 1985).

Marshall, I. Howard, *The Gospel of Luke* (Paternoster, 1978).

Mohabir, Philip, *Building Bridges* (Hodder & Stoughton,

214

1988).

Noble, John, *House Churches*: Will They Survive? (Kingsway, 1988).

Owens, Jimmy and Carol, *Come Together* (Lexicon Music, 1972).

Owens, Jimmy and Carol, *If my people* (Lexicon Music, 1974).

Pulkingham, Graham *Gathered for Power* (Hodder & Stoughton 1972).

Smail, Tom (ed.), *Gospel and Spirit: a Joint Statement* (Fountain Trust, 1977).

Springer, Kevin (ed.), *Riding the Third Wave* (Marshall Pickering, 1987).

Stott, John, *God's New Society* (IVP 1979).

Walker, Andrew, *Enemy Territory - the Christian Struggle for the Modern World* (Hodder & Stoughton, 1987).

Walker, Andrew, *Restoring the Kingdom* (Hodder & Stoughton, 1985).

Watson, David, *I believe in the Church* (Hodder & Stoughton, 1978).

Watson, David, *You Are My God* (Hodder & Stoughton, 1983).

Whittaker, Colin, *Great Revivals* (Marshalls, 1984).

215